~ *The Great Apple Raid* ~

Books by
Arthur Hopcraft

Born to Hunger
The Football Man
The Great Apple Raid

The
Great Apple Raid

&
other encounters of a
Tin Chapel Tiro

by
Arthur Hopcraft

HEINEMANN : LONDON

William Heinemann Ltd
LONDON MELBOURNE TORONTO
JOHANNESBURG AUCKLAND

First published 1970
© 1970 by Arthur Hopcraft

Printed in Great Britain by
Western Printing Services Ltd, Bristol

To my father and my late mother

Contents

❧ *Author's Note* ❧

This book is a response to memory. Some people in it have been given fictitious names. The book was suggested to me by a number of pieces I wrote for *Nova* during 1968, and some anecdotes and descriptive fragments from them reappear here.

I

Arrivals

At that age, of course, I could not have spelled 'swaddled'; could not have written down any grouping of letters to represent the sound, or recognized the word on a printed page for the human condition I associated with it. But it had a brimming potency for me. I loved the word: relished it in secret and greed, like a glassy, slow-melting peppermint sucked to a lingering end in the feathery solitude of bed. Swaddled was a contemptible thing to be, and I wasn't it.

It meant, to begin with, being encased in a great and devious winding of wool, usually a grandmotherly shawl or perhaps a couple of broad scarves stitched together, the route of this greasy and tickling maze taking it round the head, neck, shoulders, chest and stomach and ending in a vast safety pin plunged just short of the flesh at the small of the back. In these strait-jackets whole platoons of children arrived at school and steamed gently in queues at the teachers' desks, waiting to be unpinned and unravelled before they could join the rest of us less problematically clothed and already in our places. There was a distinct setting apart in this daily rite of winter. The teachers were at once tender and testy in the chore; it was apparent that they disliked it, as the children did, stiff and sullen as if under scolding. I was aloof and safe from it, because of my coat and Wellingtons and my astrakhan-backed gloves.

The mummified children were the coatless, and mostly they were the ones with the runniest noses and the too-big boots. They were also mostly the fiercest of the playground fighters, who could kick out without qualm, girls as well as boys. They were the ones who were most intimidatingly inquisitive about me, the stranger with a bar of chocolate in his pocket and a blatantly different accent. 'Why do you?' one of them had bawled in my face, and then he stepped back to allow his accomplice to hurtle into position and complete the pre-arranged, triumphant accusation: 'Have your hair cut like a girl?' I had stared speechless with bewilderment at them, who both had the all-round fringe which was uniform for boys in the district and which was known as the pudding-basin haircut and was much nearer to the way my sister had her hair than was my own parted-and-brushed-down style. 'Eez 'ad it trained,' said some big girl, confusing me further and kneeling in front of me to inspect the phenomenon. The end of playtime closed the incident but not, of course, the puzzle. I was six, I was new, I was too interesting, and too questioning, for peace of mind.

When I heard my parents discuss the belligerent, mummified children, and declare disapprovingly that they were swaddled I absorbed the word with a private hug of relief. To be swaddled was to be wrong: about haircuts, how to talk, how to play, everything. Swaddled was my first conscious curse, first judgement, first obscenity. I cuddled it in my head during those alarming first weeks in Blackfords and it gave me an exciting kind of solace.

Then the wind stopped blowing the hailstones against the tall sash windows. The shawls and the scarves were put into cupboards; and their owners, liberated, were more friendly in the sun. It had been a swaddle of a winter, but it had ended.

We had come to Blackfords, near Cannock, Staffordshire, from seaside Essex via London. I had known, before this pit village (although the word 'village' was never used and it was certainly no town), a brilliant, warm daylight, with sand seemingly always between my toes and fingers, and soldiers on huge horses to watch cantering in a smell of salt spray. I had experienced a sudden turmoil, with suit-cases and trains and hand-shaking, into which was blurred a memory of school with very tall rooms and of being one of scores of children sitting cross-legged in plimsolls on a shiny wooden floor. There had been tears of terror when an aeroplane thundered between the chimney pots, and the world went dark as my head vibrated. And I knew the word 'dug-out', which had occurred one day when a big hole was scooped in the back garden and a metallic covering put over it. Such were Essex and London. In February 1939, we were in Blackfords; and my knowing life was borne in on me in a crucial coincidence with the coming of the war.

It is surely the vital factor affecting my generation that it pursued its infancy in an environment of impending, and inexorable, conflict. That is more important, I think, than that its more robust, less ignorant childhood observed the war itself. Not understanding the conversation around me in 1939, I was certainly aware of an agitation. I remember it not as something that had specific manifestations but as a background tension, a crackly quality, which invaded places and rituals, such as the tea-table and Sunday morning church. It conveyed a need for a personal alertness, which had not been necessary before. Our infancy was heightened, sensi-tized, threatened, by something that loomed most awesomely. By so clearly worrying our parents, without showing itself, it was insidiously disturbing. If my generation is, as it is accused of being, excessively and tediously nostalgic, I feel that the reason may lie here. Our infant years were over-whelmingly significant; after so much portent most of what followed had to be anti-climax. We grew up to a habit of looking back and wondering.

But now there was Blackfords. Particularly there was The Central Corner, a redbrick promontory at the confluence of five narrow roads, on which we lived. My father was managing a bread-and-grocery shop, and our house was attached to it, gaunt and rattling, with high ceilings, damp walls and not much natural light. The shop fitted into the blunt-ended 'V' of the corner site, with the house connected to it by a thin passage, always smelling of cheese and soap and bacon, and beyond the house were the owners' covered-in vehicle yard and their bakery.

It was a curious, compelling playground for me, younger than my brother by seven years and than my sister by eighteen months and permitted an indulgently loose rein for wandering in that gloomy, cavernous warren. I could dodge among the jockeying bread vans and the flour-dusted staff when the place was at work; and when it was silent in dusky evenings and at weekends, and the shapes were distorted in the gloom, there was added a most delicious merging of fear and courage to my hide-and-seek with the cats. The bakery had a big upstairs store room stacked with bags of flour to a height about three times my own, and I would emerge from my wriggling, tunnelling explorations of this inviting forbidden ground covered in an off-white film very like the wedges of cod the moment before they were plopped into the batter in the fish and chip shop a few doors up Old Fallow Road. I once kicked a woman's shin accidentally in that shop, and after an exaggerated wail of pain she called me a little sod, which gave me much satisfaction, since it was the first time I had ever been sworn at and it seemed to me an honourable wound, overdue and surprisingly painless. In Blackfords swearing at children, very loudly, seemed to be the most common way of addressing

them in and around the home, and to have become a little
sod capable of exciting such a crescendo of anger from this
purple adult identified me, I thought, much more closely
with my contemporaries.

There was no swearing in my own home. We were
Methodists, and prominently so, my father being a lay
preacher and Sunday School teacher. The rest of us sat
unfailingly Sunday to Sunday in our pew, polished for God
and note perfect very nearly all the way through the hymn-
book.

But I now heard hymns sung in a different style and
altogether different spirit from what I was used to in the
decorous enthusiasm of chapel. Immediately across the
road on one side of our house was a pub, and about three
hundred yards away was a working men's club, and from
both there would come on Saturday and Sunday nights the
bellowed, swooping, slurred choruses of every working-
class drunk's favourite hymn. 'Guide me, oh thou great
Jehovah, pilgrim through this barren land,' it began, and the
words and tune permitted a relentless dragging which
could bring a besotted chorister to tears or set on edge the
teeth of any sober man with an ounce of musicality. Then
there was the hymn's resounding refrain, with its emphatic
monosyllables, which could tempt men already tight to
bursting point with pints of mild to catapult their soft
palates at the ceiling: 'Bread of He-he-ven, Bread of
He-he-ven, Feed me now and ever more. . . .'

I would lie in bed and hear this rolling and rollicking
sound, massively reverberative when the singers were
collected and static in the bars, more lurching and ragged
when they were on their hesitant way home past the house
in small groups. Drunkenness was new to me too. Under the
weighty eiderdown in the bed with the shiny brass turnips
screwed into the posts I was protected and I giggled, and I

distorted my pretty little treble into an impersonation given
a peculiar muffled sonority by the tent of wool and feathers:
'Bread of He-he-ven, Bread of He-he-ven . . .' Blackfords
was strange, irreverent, improper to me; and exciting.

Going to school was the overriding interest: not, that is,
what occurred in the classroom but what surrounded it in
the streets and punctuated it in the playground. In class we
handled officialdom's toys: coloured crayons, coloured
paper, bright beads threaded on wires in frames, little
mirrors to talk at and watch the movements of our lips and
tongues as we formed round vowels and sharp Ts and Ds
and ringing Gs. But the effective education was imparted
on the asphalt and along the hunched terraces and under the
hicky-hawthorn hedges. Here I met the brave, the sad and
the mad.

The walk to Chadsmoor Infants was about half a mile,
and in that short space we had a world: commerce, derelic-
tion, poverty, wealth, and the beauty and claw of nature.
The route went out of the bakery yard and past the sour
door of the pub where, on a bearably warm morning, men
would already be crouched in the miner's way, backside
against the wall and elbows resting on knees, a position that
agonizes men of any other occupation within minutes and
which the pitmen would hold in coughing contemplation
for hours; across the road past the other grocer's, and then
the garage with the gleaming bicycles in the showroom;
then past the long, blood-black terrace where some of those
swaddled children lived, with the piles of miners' con-
cessionary coal outside the doors and women with bleak,
thin faces and torn shoes scouring doorsteps and yelling
swearwords at each other in a smell of old mattresses; then,
instantly, the tough, tangled and entrancingly mysterious
hedgerow, the leaves mauve with dust but with birds and
bugs among them with the thrown-away bits of old clothing,

and dogs that came raging through the branches from the field behind, going for your ankles or for the spitting cats with coats like frayed coconut mats; then Scrappy Evans's reeking and clanking yard heaped with junk, orange with rust, slime-green with mildew, blue and sickening with bonfires of the worthless, and inhabited by glamorous, filthy, gypsy-like men with neckerchiefs and big-buckled belts and sledge-hammers in brown fists; the Baptist church, squat and prim and padlocked; another terrace with a dark echoing alley you could squeal and shout in, to annoy the tenants; then the off-licence, whose proprietor was accepted to be vastly rich because he owned a car and was known already to be prepared to pay his two sons' way through grammar school if they failed the scholarship, even though it was three or four years off yet; past, very quickly and with nervous glances over the shoulder, the Big Boys' school with its stockade of railings; and then Cecil Street, and journey's end.

The daily thrill of that walk never palled. Sometimes it was made alone, sometimes with friends in a scuffling, staggered progress which called for a furious dash over the last hundred yards to avoid being late. The weather could change its character utterly, again and again. A tumult of wind would sweep the street clear of all loiterers, force us to cling together in a teetering huddle, and ram coal dust into our mouths and eyes. On the grim rainy days when every surface wept and the dogs sniffed, sorry and wheedling, round our wet socks, the place communicated a helpless exhaustion, all its dirt and scars deepened, not bathed away, by that sooty drizzle. When there was fog there was an unnerving stillness that I hardly dared to break, trying to tread silently, watching my breath undulate on that grey surface and marvelling over the fuzzy lattice-work of the transformed hedge, the hammerblows in Scrappy's yard subdued as if a mile away. On the airless summer days, when we were bare limbed and as light as corks, and cats stretched blind drunk on window sills and the dandelions were like sunflowers, we were half wild with our vitality, chased butterflies and stumbled over dozing men's legs, fought each other with stinging nettles, rattled letter-boxes, licked the salt on our own flesh and found it as delicious as sherbet.

The infants' school, where I spent about eighteen months, bordered one corner of a sloping playground, at the top of which was the Big Girls' school. As we grew older in the infants' building we became more bold, more inquisitive, about these variously heavy, stringy, shrieking, sobbing figures in jumpers and skirts, who seemed to spend most of their playtime upside down with their hands on the ground and the soles of their feet up against the wall, skirts dangling round their chins. Sometimes we observed one of their teachers, furiously angry about something, rushing into a little group of the girls, now upright, with their heads together, and bellowing that she wouldn't have it. These girls were up to the age of fourteen. We heard that these outbursts were all to do with 'talking', which explained nothing at all.

From time to time, in my last months with the infants, our teacher took to shaking her head at us sorrowfully, usually when one of us wanted to go to the lavatory, and saying: 'I don't know *what*'s going to happen to you when you get to the Big Boys.' That was ominous enough by itself; but when it was added to the puzzling alarms up the playground at the Big Girls there seemed to be something frightful awaiting us on our arrival at bigness. No talking, no widdling, or else. The functions seemed guiltless. Time would re-educate us.

For the moment we said what we liked and let our widdle

rip, describing our initials with it, those of us who had
mastered the art, on the furry lavatory wall, and took
pleasure in the flourish. We developed other skills, as well.
We had enough co-ordination for football now, and the
intense satisfaction, quite like meeting an innate urge, of
connecting the right foot in a firm slap with the rubber ball,
caught luckily but truly on the half-volley, was memorably
one of the key experiences of my first eight years of life.

One of my friends could hurtle through spectacular
cartwheels and intuitively self-taught back-flips, unconcerned at the danger in the playground surface. I recognized in
him a reckless physical courage which I sensed had to do
with the casual toughness of his home, its poverty and his
mixture of sluggish literacy and instant aggressiveness,
because he was my opposite in all these things and I certainly could not match his cartwheels. His name was John,
he was dressed usually in obvious cut-downs, his nose ran
like a leak in a roof-gutter and he had the prominent, fleshless
shin-bones, cheek-bones and knuckles of the hard life. We
had a brief, inquiring, watchful friendship, intrigued by
each other's strangeness, a situation perhaps best summarized
by his considered statement to me, after a prolonged sniff
of that free-flowing nose: 'Yo talk posh.' He was not the
most accurate spitter in the school; there was someone else
who, I think because of an unusual grouping of his front
teeth, could employ a kind of hissing, snake-like ejection to
land slime on your face from any distance he chose. But
John was the best thrower, the right arm, thin as a stair-rod,
clenching and jack-knifing straight with a savage power.
We were tiny, frail and formidable; anarchists despising,
ignoring, and relying on, adults.

They could sometimes jerk us out of our collective self-
absorption: by an unintended comicality, perhaps, as in an old
miner's crippled and wavering walk, the easy and rhythmic

springiness of the knees that the younger ones had being
grotesquely distorted by age and injury so that his legs
assumed random angles and bends, coming together and
parting without control; or by sudden anger erupting in
circumstances inappropriate to it. One of these inexplicable
moments occurred in a sweetshop, one of the stuffy little
terrace-house, front-room shops near the school, when an
urgent gaggle of us blustered in, banging our heads against
the tins and jars, shrieking in argument about what to buy.
We settled uniformly on flat sticks of toffee, a ha'penny each,
since volume was especially attractive and deviation from
majority decision highly suspect. Everyone produced a
penny and rushed out with two sticks until I broke the
pattern by thrusting out twopence, being unprecedently
rich for a weekday, and said I would have four. The shopkeeper was a heavy woman of particularly morose, droopy
character; she had a row of nasty little canes clicking their
teeth together on a string above the chocolate drops and
aniseed balls, and their presence always gave her place an
atmosphere of threat: reward and retribution joined
trickily in conspiracy. I would never go in there alone. The
woman was visibly jolted when I spoke, immediately expan-
ding in every direction, and she made the shelves rattle
when she answered. 'You'll 'ave *two*,' she bawled. 'Like
everyone *else*.' And she added the preposterous impre-
cation: '*Yo* and all yer money.'

The charge was unanswerable, of course, since there was
a general assumption in my circle that my family was well-
to-do, which was a total misconception. It was our style
that was the trouble: our careful, southern voices, gloves and
clean handkerchiefs, my father's raised position in the
pulpit, my mother's custom of invariably referring to him
in the presence of non-family as 'Mr Hopcraft', which was a
known discretion of respectability and contrasted glaringly

with the offhand way my friends' parents cast first names about or referred simply to 'im' and 'er'.

We had arrived in this community on the shoves and shrugs of the Depression, my father having disposed of the debris of his own small grocery business, and my mother spruced us and nurtured us with a leisureless attention to detail on an income that allowed no frivolity whatever with the small change. But our austerity was not the conditioned poverty of the miners' families, who had inherited intermittent unemployment, insecure wages and a sense of ordained deprivation along with the men's crippling work underground.

I knew very quickly after we arrived that the women bought food cheaply by habit, and I could see at first glances that furniture and clothing and general standards of comfort were more coarse, less considered, than our own. My father was ideally placed behind his counter to observe local living standards, and I was always, from first consciousness, a natural, avid eavesdropper and interrogator.

My parents had both been brought up mostly in southern country villages, where they also had their early married life, and their attitudes were informed by a thrifty but robust, open-skied security. There were always gardens and pony traps and harvests and gentry with servants in their reminiscence. Listening so intently, I was bound to be aware of a difference between their past and our present. But I was just as fascinated, indeed more so, by this new place of long, hemmed-in streets, where the sun would thrust in a burning arrowhead for an instant and ignite a musty window, then withdraw to leave it in ashes, and where ferocious abuse would explode through closed doors – a shrill torrent, a masculine bellow, a scream, a blur of criss-crossing movement behind a net curtain, then stillness – and where the black of coal dominated everything with a harsh and sombre royalty.

I assimilated these memories, sights, sounds and smells, and let them ripple and entwine within me. Knowledge and mystery collided, fused, fragmented and re-grouped in uneasy, shared occupation of my never-still mind. I accepted for myself a condition of exclusion not resented, because the circumstances were not oppressive, but noted undeniably as something that could not be overcome in those streets. 'You and all your money,' I knew was nonsense, because money was seldom seen in anything but tiny amounts. Yet there had been a pointing out, a recognition of my non-member-ship, in that outburst. I was closely attached, but did not belong.

Was it this sense of strangeness, a painless enough singularity, that attracted me so much to some other non-members, the figures with the long heads and leaning walks, supporting themselves against invisible walls in the air, who made their drooling progress up the path outside the playground to the building facing the girls' school? These were the children described for us as 'simple', 'mental' or 'backward'. We were told not to stare at them, and to keep clear. They were dreamlike people to me, their slow and puzzled movements lacking reference to the normal order and precision around them. Their unreality intrigued me. I assumed, of course, that they were peculiar to the district, but also that they all lived together somewhere, and I was astonished when a boy I knew well pointed to his sister among them.

The revelation unsettled my non-committal interest in them. If they were part of real families and yet so different they were altogether more questionable, in the disapproving sense, than I had at first thought. The word 'daft' was used frequently about them. It was also used towards me and my friends when we became unbearably rowdy or sulky, or in any other minor way irritating to older people. On these occa-

sions we always knew that we were deliberately misbehaving,
so I came to believe for a while that the simple children
conducted themselves in their odd, wayward manners by
their own design, flouting the instructions about speaking
clearly and standing up straight which constrained the rest
of us. The problem was whether to admire or condemn this
rebellion. I made a couple of attempts to talk to them, was
given a dribbling grin and some jerky words I could not
frame into meaning, and was abruptly dragged away by a
teacher who seemed very flustered. My uncertainty hung on
unresolved, and with it a suppressed kind of sympathy
which would sometimes grow into a hankering to be like them:
pretending helplessness, unapproachable by choice, showing
blind eyes and deaf ears to the world, and yet, as I thought,
seeing and hearing all.

I suppose this fantasy was an extension of my belief in
my detachment. To be free to enter and reject the daily
world at will appealed enormously: the infant's, fingers-over-
eyes game of 'I'll wake up when I'm ready,' greatly ela-
borated. But there was something more there than that, I
feel. The element of disguise was such an attraction: to be
able to fathom and know every detail of a world that teemed
with new curiosities and not to be obstructed, because of
being disregarded. Wasn't there a favourite story about a
prince leaving his palace dressed like one of the lower orders
and mingling, fascinated and unconsidered, among the
beggars and the thieves?

Now that I could read fluently I was insatiable for new
heroes, and I enjoyed jumbling quick transferences of
character into my reasoning in this way. It was a heady,
dangerous game, when I played it in my mind in adults'
presence, because I had to rely on my mental agility to step
instantly back into the real world when spoken to. The
droning multiplication tables and pizzicato rhymes, for

instance, had to be given a misty attention on the perimeter of my fantasies, sufficient for a slick link-up the moment the teacher's pointer cued me in. My arrogance towards school work at this stage was an amused, snug pleasure. I could spell, count, recite, with easy accuracy, and it was clear that I was much admired. Girls hugged me.

But there arrived stealthily, so that no precise moment can be given to it, a time when this self possession, this ordering of life to my whim and curiosity, came to an end. I found I was involved with others, that I had to give them reasons for actions, that I was affected by events, that I had lost my callousness and could observe pride and guilt both in myself and other people. The free animal of me, with its primal cunning, had evolved. I knew the streets, people's names and habits, knew whom I could bully and who could bully me, and whom I could manipulate, and why. The present, the very instant, had become a challenge, not just a fascinating fact.

I was out of the Infants and in the daily conflict, so much more vital than that other, soldiers' war in the background, of the scheming life.

2

Factors

War was declared on Blackfords, regardless of when it had arrived elsewhere, on the same night that Robin Hood and the Black Prince settled their differences with jousting lances upside down on my bedroom ceiling. One moment I was promising to fight the winner, the next I was being hustled upright and wrapped in a blanket in the up-and-down snarl of a siren and deposited in an irritable daze on top of the linen chest on the landing.

There was a great deal of heavy breathing from my parents, who were also talking in peculiar rapid snatches, their voices unusually low. The lights were off, but there were candles with wavery flames. I suddenly became aware of a distant thudding, like something heavy falling on a carpet, except that this noise was repeated over and over. Then the candles were blown out and the curtain at the landing window opened, and in the sky great beams of white light stood out like luminous clock fingers. The whole family, huddled in our slippers, stared at a slow-moving firework display whose explosions were faint and whose white and orange flashes were no greater than the spurt of a safety match. Yet it was clearly an important occasion. That prickly tension was in the air again, and our faces were taut and yellowy against the grey of the window.

The searchlight beams were the brightest of the lights. I liked the way they veered across the sky, converging coyly, kissing and parting. The thudding continued, and it was a muffled interference, because of its lack of settled rhythm, with the lullaby of my breathing when the lights began to bore and we went back to our makeshift beds at the top of the stairs.

The war proved principally a disturbance of sleep. The air raids on Birmingham and Coventry were far enough away never to endanger us physically. But they discomfited naggingly, unsettling the order of the house. We never once went to the air raid shelter which had been dug and sandbagged in the big recreation field with the tall wooden gates next to the butcher's shop. Some families had gone to it, so we heard, on the first one or two nights of alarm, but felt insufficiently menaced to continue the precaution. We moved beds about according to some logic beyond my understanding. Sometimes I was on the landing, sometimes I woke up astonished in the living-room. The objective, it seemed, was to be prepared: for a quick exit, presumably. To be prepared. Again there was that imprecise, nodded-at, sighed-about, intimation of disaster, of which we were not to be frightened, yet we were to look out for it all the same. But no bombs fell on Blackfords.

Indeed we were, we discovered after all, a comparative haven of safety. Other places sent evacuees to us: a straggle of raincoats and cardboard boxes hanging on string from thin necks, and occasioning a sense of communal guilt:

'Like picking out cattle at the market.'

'Poor little sods.'

'It's a shame.'

'May God forgive them.'

'You 'aven't 'ad to leave yer mum and dad, *'ave* yer?'

Abruptly a new ritual had invaded the day. It was called The News, and it imposed a silence as deep as that accorded a preacher's sermon. One o'clock, six o'clock, nine o'clock:

the grave, well-off voice was not to be interrupted by the clink of a spoon or the rustle of a paper bag or the creak of a chair. It was the voice of the wireless, impeccably punctual, noble with aitches, dominating. It delivered unquestionable truths about *aircrahft* and *advahnces* and the *High C'mahnd*. It did not lead to discussion afterwards. The family, and whoever among neighbours and friends were augmenting the audience at the time, gave that voice more than a religious observance. It was a more immediately intimidating sound of war than the distant explosions.

Like the evacuees we had our gas-masks: a touch of cold rubber, a stranglehold from behind, a disconcerting smell suggesting fainting, a game with bits of paper held by suction to the mask's wobbling, perforated chin.

There were daytime air raid drills at school, when we marched to the shelters, but not often. The shelters were pitch dark, and we were first frightened, then defiant, then riotous, teachers bawling in cracking voices for order and obedience, threatening ferocious punishment, shining torches, counting us, losing us, as we scrambled and hid in the vindictive glee of our unexpected opportunity for seizing a few minutes of power.

We would spill from the dank, foetid tunnel like a froth of Tizer out of a shaken-up bottle, our minders vexed by dust and plaster and spiders in their hair and gripped by the trembles, blowing their whistles and countermanding each other's orders in a confusion that was joy to us. The drill would bring an end to the day; we would be released early to pelt for the back lanes and hedges, tipsy celebrants of freedom retrieved, while those flushed women and muttering men hunted the causes of their meandering itches and cursed us and Hitler.

Soldiers appeared in the streets, down in the town near the churchyard, slouchy and arrogant when on their own,

awkward and twitch-eyed when formed up and being
bellowed at by sergeants. The women of the district were
definitely on the side of the squads, and disapproving of the
sergeants:

'Ah, the poor devils.'

'Shurrup, yo ratty bugger.'

'I never could abide a man with a ratty face.'

'It's enough to make yo blart, ay it?'

That seemed to me to be overstating the case. Blarting,
which was crying, was something to be avoided if at all
possible, and the remedy here appeared to be for the
squads to employ their superior strength of number to
overwhelm the shouting sergeants; or, for that matter, for
the women to do it, since there were enough of them. The
rebellion did not occur. The infantry marched away, its
boots making a disappointingly thin sound, compared to
that of the miners walking home with no-one to call the step
but with a greater unity in that patient, iron-booted trudge,
faces smeared with coal dust, thumbs hanging on the belts
sagging well below their waists. The soldiers were only
brief visitors to Blackfords' war; the miners fought in a
conflict that had its lulls but could have no end.

Suddenly there were tanks. They deafened a morning,
huge in the narrow streets, grating and grinding at our
temples, making the windows judder, bringing people
hurrying from washtubs and chicken huts. The tanks left
behind them light-grey indentations in the gutters and a
thoughtful muttering about unstoppable power. The tanks
were subduing. Their noise had been much greater than
that of the far-away bombs, and they had an ugliness, an
unmistakably malevolent purpose in all their weight and
armour and costly, complicated engineering. They had
brutality.

In my memory the tanks and the miners' ambulance are

always immediately associated, the two fading into each other. It may possibly have the simple explanation that I saw both on the same day, perhaps the one very quickly after the other. But I do not think that is the case. The miners' ambulance had the special significance of not being like a normal ambulance which was known to be equipped for receiving the sick and the injured in some attempt at gentleness. The miners' ambulance was a rigid, dark, square-cornered vehicle, which jolted and jarred along with much the same harsh indifference as the tanks; it was known to be connected with maiming and death in dirt and noise, among cutting edges and explosions and cascading lumps of earth. This vehicle, which was sometimes a hearse with a dirty corpse still warm in it, darkened my spirit as the tanks had done. It too had brutality. It too was a war vehicle, but in that other, perpetual war with the tyranny of circumstance.

This new war could be funny. Our Sundays were some-times made giggly beyond even the stern restraint of grey preachers with hypnotic adam's apples and the wagging fingers of parents, who wedged vast like vertical sofas beside us in the chapel pew. Familiar figures, wide and waddling or long and loping, variously bulging and stick-like in Home Guard khaki, were too ludicrous to escape derision. To know they were the cause of all that muffled shouting outside, those nervous warning barks before some trivial splutter and bang, was deliciously absurd. If we were lucky we could be out of church in time to see the last moments of the manoeuvres, the portly and gangling figures, with glasses and trailing boot laces, huffing and puffing around some bit of spare ground or a derelict house, shouting George-is-dead and You're-my-prisoner and simultaneously raising their hats to our mothers, and looking dafter than Jellyman, the mythical idiot of our playground lore.

Mr Churchill's war was always more of a suppressed

scare, a bogy too terrible for identification, than a present
terror. Its early excitements and peculiarities lost their
potency, and soon most of them vanished altogether, as
with air raid drills, the majority of the evacuees, and gas
masks. We settled with a valued expertise into the night-
time blackout, catlike in the dark streets, unthreatened by
road traffic because it was so rare, knowledgeable about
radio singers and comedians and the names of aeroplanes.
We were accustomed to queues and the greasy feel of food
ration books on our errands. We were aware of this war as a
dark force whose villainy we had somehow luckily, or
divinely, been spared. Occasionally a black patch, usually
in diamond shape, would appear on a family's coat sleeves
to show that a father or a brother had been killed by that
force; but not often, because most of the men were under
ground.

The war was never as large on my consciousness as the
pits were, with the imagery they conjured of cramped wet
catacombs and men on their knees in them, half slaves, half
Guy Fawkses. Yet the war informed everything, from my
jokes to my diet; I never much considered where either
came from.

It was not long before the nocturnal displacements, the
truculent awakenings while the bombs rained on the unfortunate thirty miles away, were ended. The war went abroad.
Order and routine returned, and against their reliability
there flourished the intrigues, alliances, heroics and betrayals
which constituted the extraordinary process of adding month
to month and inch to inch.

Mr Sedgwick was as old as Abraham, although he wore
tweed suits like ragged winter privet instead of white robes,
and he visited on us a wrath that roared and whacked in a
stink of stale pipe bowls and sick-bed breath. He had a sea-

monster's moustache, and gorilla's hairs on his fists, and he
walked with a jutting motion of the head and shoulders, like
a dray-horse tugging up a hill. His reputation for classroom
violence was something we knew about long before we sat
and shivered in front of him. It seemed to have been handed
down through the generations for eternity. It was as if he
had invented the stick.

Its hooked end curled furtively over the top of the cupboard door, its length and weight concealed inside and with
a cache of other weapons, we assumed, but hardly dared
guess about them. School was a serious matter now, requiring a cowed attentiveness, all inventions banished
from the mind to make room for the cold, official verities
of I-before-E-except-after-C and Three-into-two-won't-go.
There was no time for puzzling, wondering, speculating.
'Answer, boy!' and the great brown hand slapped the desk
so that the inkwell slurped and the pen jumped in its runnel.
When the cane made its first full-length appearance,
amazingly isolated among the books and paste pots, it
swung gently against the cupboard door, yellow, fat and
curved, limbering up, as it seemed.

The man used it as if trying to chop off the hand held out
to him, rigid from the shoulder. The victim got an extra
blow if he moved. The rest of us watched frightened and
unpleasantly thrilled, treacherously collusive with Sedgwick
and avid for the sobs and welts. I do not recall any compas-
sion. There was always fear in that classroom, the most
trivial tasks, like writing down one's name and address on
instruction, made to appear like an ambush. Sufficient tension
having been created, mistakes could be induced among the
slower wits at the tyrant's will. His autarchy was exploited
with unbreachable cunning. He seemed to know about the
dark, smouldering, playtime conspiracies, when the names
of older, working brothers would be used as likely rescuers,

stepping into our abject little world and punishing the oppressor, like the Lone Ranger on a white horse. But he squashed such hopes with a withering finality. 'You're as dense as your daft brother used to be,' he would bellow in the appropriate face, abruptly diminishing that previously heroic figure to our own status of stuttering, scabby-kneed helplessness.

Old Sedgwick was a great gardener, always to be seen outside school hours with his arms full of spades and rakes or big red pots with unfamiliar leaves growing out of them. He apparently had an absorption and persuasiveness in growing plant life that was most alarmingly distorted in his dealings with small boys. He treated us rather like cabbage blight, I suppose: search for every blemish and smite it along with every suspect.

He could hardly be called an insidious influence. He coarsened us by immediate example. We had a playground chasing game, which owed a lot to his teaching. We twisted our scarves in conflicting directions, brought the two ends together and the scarf promptly entwined itself into a surprisingly stiff stick, looking like a curly chair-leg. One of the numerous circles painted on the ground was used as one team's safety area, and the other team had another. The two teams then rushed after each other, swinging away at legs and bodies with the chair-legs. The object was victory-by-ordeal. You were eliminated the moment you fled from the chase into the haven of the painted circles. There could be a distinct viciousness here. If a team was overmanned by the timid its braver members would rapidly be greatly out-numbered, and the blows would fall with venom, while the drop-outs in the circle watched and gasped.

'Ooh, that one was 'arder than Mr Sedgwick.'

There was always a great deal of punching and wrestling among us; but this game had an unusual formality, an imitative, take-your-medicine character. It was stopped one day when someone replaced his scarf with a belt he could wrap round himself twice, and he produced a weal like a fried egg on another boy's leg. The word for that situation nowadays, I suppose, is escalation. We called it cheating, and it created such a stir that one of the women teachers had the scarf game banned.

Fortunately Sedgwick the Terrible was not the only important figure in the primary school. We seemed to be in and out of his class, probably because of other teachers' illnesses, so that he recurred in my life very like a sinister dream, wrinkling through his moustache and barking: 'Back again, eh? You won't have it soft here!' The hands would clap together like house bricks. The voice clanked on our wincing heads like swipes with a bucket.

But there was also Mr Lubbock, who was as tall as the classroom doors, with a white thin face and red thin nose. He was altogether a gentler proposition than Mr Sedgwick. He read to us a lot, although not very excitingly; it was a case of the intention being welcomed as much more significant than the material. He seemed definitely to like us; would often carry the smaller figures on his shoulders, which was a hazardous experience because his great height meant that the passenger had to duck to avoid meeting the lintels with his throat. There was a lot of laughter in Mr Lubbock's class, and there was chatter about football and birds' nests. We worked hard at keeping him amiable, and threw him from our minds the moment we were clear of the classroom, which was not a prize we awarded old Sedgwick.

We also had Miss Crockett, whose neck was like half a white drainpipe and who sat on her huge slow bicycle, basketed front and back, with a shoulders-braced, nodding serenity: Queen Mary economizing on the gilded coach for the war effort. We recognized efficiency in her; she taught us matters that stayed in our minds. A stitch in time saved nine, prevention was better than cure, Spitfires won the Battle of Britain, Lazarus was raised from the dead, A times B equals AB. Eh? She had overestimated us there, even the little knot of geniuses who wore monitors' badges and were going to pass the scholarship for her. One letter *times* another letter? Bewilderment. Incomprehension. Resentment. Miss Crockett tinkled with her encouraging, kindly laugh, and said: 'There are more things in heaven and earth, boys, than you've ever dreamed of.'

She supervised our football, with a real leather ball known as a casey, and shepherded us off to the public park where there were stretches of soft grass, we trotting in an earnest column on the pavement, she undulating discreetly on her bicycle. She knew quite a lot about football, deciding without hesitation on corners and penalties and rising appreciably in our regard. In her high, thin voice she called the order of the game with an unstinted enthusiasm: 'Raight then, the Reds,' (we wore coloured sashes to denote the team) 'it's a goalla-keek for you. Give it a good besh, John.'

She wore us out:

'Miss, can I 'ave a drinkapop?' A dash for the bicycle, representing one conjunction of touchline and half-way-line, and the pile of coats beside it protecting the lemonade: great gulpings at the warm, frothing bottle, feet lashing out as the ball came rolling close, and going boss-eyed trying to watch the bottle and the ball at once. 'Reely, Walter, such a baby. Hend ball there, William. Free keek for the Blews.'

The headmaster undertook the artistic aspects of our education. He was a natty man with plenty of dark hair shining with grease, and he was always urging us to take much more pride in how we scrubbed our visible flesh. He once worked his way through the whole class asking everyone how long we thought a well-groomed headmaster should

spend in front of the mirror every morning preparing himself for the world's critical eye. I offered the figure of 40
seconds, on the silent reasoning that a man accustomed to the
task would need next to no time, and he gave me an ad-
monishing frown.

He was an artist and a musician. The walls of his study
were hung with his caricatures of men, each of whom had
been given Christian names. I once had the chance to hunt
for 'Arthur', and was not pleased to find a flaccid figure with
a bow tie. But it was singing that brought the headmaster's
personality exploding into bloom. He played the piano with
a swanking flourish, the hands hitting the keys from
shoulder height, and he would force his voice to drown his
choir's and prove that we were not really trying for the *brio*
he was demanding. He wrote a school song, whose chorus
went: 'Play up and play the game, It's the only thing to do.'

'Linden Lea' was a favourite in his repertoire, and I
agreed with him in enjoying its broad, simple melody, and I
delighted in mastering the tricky last words of the chorus:
'. . . To where for me, The apple tree, Do lean down low,
In Linden Lea.' But he excited us most with the least
suitable of his songs for boys' treble voices, a sort of concert
Negro folk song, all about 'One more kiss for Dinah, dear,'
and having a captivatingly trite finale: 'Hark, it is de
oberseer, Steal away and so good night, Good night (dimin-
uendo), *Good night*. He would allow us to bawl the last
line.

He took this singing with a seriousness which could
sometimes be disturbing. I was once sent by one of the
teachers to interrupt him during a singing lesson with
another class, and ask for some sheets of coloured paper. He
yelled, 'Get off my stage,' and threw me at the front row of
the singers.

The performance was something I later came to recognize

as an outburst of artistic temperament. Great orchestral conductors, I learned, sometimes flung their batons at inaccurate triangle players, and painters cut their own ears off in frustration when life irritated them. Clearly our headmaster was a man burdened by the demands of his own greatness, although in that case, I thought, ought he not to be on the wireless with Webster Booth and Myra Hess? No doubt this misplacement was due to the war.

He trained us for a concert we gave in the Baptist church, and the place was packed with watch chains and pink hats. We engendered in this audience a sloppy cooing when we had finished. I was used to singing in choirs, because of Sunday School, but not to this response, which seemed overdone and embarrassing. We were having our heads patted, and adults were fussing and sniffing over us. We had sung, 'There'll Always Be an England' in our solemn sopranos; the war was at its height.

Between Miss Crockett and Mr Coote, the headmaster, was a chasm of difference in terms of contrasting sensibility. With her we were introduced to Mole and Toad of Toad Hall and discovered a ready tenderness in ourselves that was strangely connected with laughter. Her classroom was animated in a special chirrupy way, to do with polite nimbleness. She was my definitive spinster; a clean, little-mouthed face framed by catkins in milk bottles.

With Mr Coote we were persuaded towards embellishment. He was a show-off, and he hurried us into his kind of florid facility. His ear was quick for a tune or someone else's accent. 'Come on, you've seen Wallace Beery at the pictures,' he would say, as we acted out the decline and fall of Cyclops, using the big teacher's desk for a cave or a headland, and he would lurch through a fair impersonation of Beery's punched-up face and walk and way of talking.

We were not sure about our headmaster. He appeared

only at intervals from his dark and secretive study next door
to the cloakroom, and we were principally an audience for
him instead of a class; uncritical, of course. But he gave us a
lot of tunes and rhymes which stayed with us outside school.
One of my friends said to me: 'My dad says Mr Coote's a
pansy.' I had no idea, and none of us had, what that careless
slander implied, but there was something most effectively
descriptive about the word – its sound much more than its
reference to a very dinky flower – that fitted the face and the
personality. He was my definitive pansy: a smooth-faced
adult male with a breast pocket handkerchief and bouncy
movements accompanied by song.

Catastrophe struck in a blast of red-hot itching powder
from a shotgun. It woke me up one morning in a panic
compounded by the evident alarm and distaste in the
expressions of the rest of the family as they hurried in to
stare at me. My face had taken the brunt of this monstrous
assault, but stray pellets had caught my hands as well. The
mirror showed an image like congealed hundreds-and-
thousands sweets in gigantic proportions. I was a pebbledash
jelly.

The name of the ammunition the night-time assailant had
used, I discovered, was Impetigo. It gave me one of my
most celebrated sicknesses.

For one thing it brought into the life of the household a
beguilingly beautiful being known as The Little Nurse. She
was indeed tiny, an angel-girl, a Snow White in a navy-blue
gaberdine, with hands like feathers and an equally weightless
body movement matched by a voice that danced in the air.
I was speechlessly in love, staring, gaping, limp and obedient
as she breathed balm over me with silver chatter that had no
meaning except a flawless loveliness. She would arrive with
a delicate tap of gloved fingertips on the back door, a gush

of welcome from my mother, a skipping glide across the linoleum and the mats to my repulsive presence, and with her glinting eyes and laughter she would rekindle my self-respect in my renewed adoration of her. I was a leper; she embraced me.

The ghastly blotches broke and drained down my cheeks, and yellow crusts like dead buttercup heads replaced them, sticky and adhesive and magnetically pickable. My mother made mittens out of some silk and fastened them round my wrists to reduce the self-inflicted damage. I was the reason for much special activity of many kinds. I had to be washed as if a baby, cups and plates and spoons were set aside for me, towels and face flannels were reserved for my exclusive use. I was inspected with diminishing displeasure. But I saw less of Snow White, as my features reappeared from behind their peppery mask.

School all but vanished from my mind. In silk gloves and with a marble whiteness to my forehead I was allowed out into the gust and shadow of the spring streets. I felt too old for the tricycle, that magical acquisition from an ancient Christmas, so tied string to the handlebars to use as reins and add a difficulty and danger to the steering suitable to my advancing years; and I pedalled round the re-awakened world.

I seemed to be the only child alive. At eleven o'clock in the morning and three o'clock in the afternoon, hours of mobile freedom unknown to me except at weekends and during the squealing, pell-mell school holidays, I was the solitary survivor of my extinct kind. I wandered three-wheeled through the alleyways and over the gritty spare ground, kicking imperiously at the surprised dogs, speeding suddenly into a shimmering pewter haze of dust lit by the sun across a gap in a terrace, labouring to a roll of drums in my head up to the crown of some hill, then wheeling, waiting for the pistol crack and hurtling to the bottom, standing in the stirrups with wind and trumpets in my ears.

I was in a two-dimensional world; it had movement and colour but very little sound. Motor traffic was minimal, the rag-and-bone men clip-clopped skinnily by on their pony-pulled beds of pillow stuffing and fire fenders; and black Higgie, the coalman, glowered in his metal-studded leather coat behind his dawdling Clydesdale – a magnificent, barbaric partnership of muscle and whip; and always the off-work miners, with bandaged heads and hands, crouched against the walls with their pallid, pitted faces shut and silent as they conserved their resilience for the pains to come. All my own sounds were sharp and important in these torpid hours: my sniffs, swallowings, sweet-suckings, footsteps, defined like the clugging and clicking of some purposeful engine. My purpose was simply to move; I was quick among sloth.

But some kind of spell was on me. Restored to the urgent timetable of arithmetic and nature study and cementing friendships and poisoning other people's, I was felled again and again by brief, unprecedented agonies and contagions: stomach, throat, stomach, in turn sand-papered and then speared by fire. Horizontal and stunned, I seemed to be shrivelling while the family loomed larger by the hour. Flesh and bone melted into the air; I was nothing but a half-open mouth in a white smell of vomit.

The recoveries from these miseries were deeply mysterious. First would come a sudden ability to smile, then to sing, and then an extraordinary acceleration in the workings of the senses. Household sounds reached me ahead of the activity I knew would cause them; the smell of gravy arrived at its mention, the taste of apple pudding on sight of the empty dish it was to be cooked in. To clench a fist was to

create a surge of sensuous power; to be back in the wind
kicking a ball was a swaggering triumph.

The cycle had its climax: a flurry of smiles and re-
assurances, a short journey in a small bus to white tiles and
medicine smells, an obedient deep breath, and the ceiling
pushing down on me like black velvet; and waking up in a
writhing whimpering of other children on a line of mattresses; and a man in a peaked cap carrying me; and a totally
disinterested mental observation that I was intact from feet
to shoulders but that I did not have a head.

' Have I been run over, Mum?'

'No, you've had your tonsils out. Like we told you.'

'Is that all, though?'

'I've made you some lemonade. The kind you like. From
the crystals.'

'Does everybody else have their tonsils out?'

'The Little Nurse is coming to see you tomorrow.'

I knew now that I still possessed a head because it reeled
slightly at the mention of Snow White's title. I planned for
her coming, shock and resentment at the puzzling and
hurting ill-treatment of the immediate past dissipated in an
intermittent, pain-punctuated way by my relish of the
delight ahead.

She came to my bed in a glistening serenade. I was wan and
broken and entreating on my pillow. Soup and lemonade
were holding me back from the jaws of death. Her caress
and the cool perfume of her breath would revive me, as long
as both were long and frequently applied.

She looked and giggled, smiled and dimpled, touched my
forehead and nodded her curls. 'I've just come from one
little girl who's sitting up eating fish and chips,' she said,
and she straightened her hat and skipped away and was never
seen again; not that I cared any more, since she'd gone ugly
all of a sudden. And strict.

3

Football, Film Stars, Hallelujah!

We moved one day, about a hundred yards and into a different plane. We went across the road from the front of the shop, so that it was now between us and the pub, past the cinema and the tin chapel and to the semi-detached house immediately the other side of the chapel railings. At the shop there had not been a garden; now we had a square one at the front and a rectangular one at the back, with a sloping lawn and apple trees, a dead pear tree, wallflowers, hollyhocks much taller than I was, stone steps beside the lawn and secret, olive corners, damp and dark and dungeon-acrid in their concealment from the sun.

The garden was of disproportionate grandeur for a modest house with an outside lavatory. It had paths I could kick a ball round; we could play hide-and-seek in it. It was just like a country garden, my parents said, with thickets of flowers, tunnels of runner-beans, marrow-beds with their magically creeping tendrils, tufted quilts of strawberries and a potato patch to feed an army. Suddenly our home life was swooning with flowers. The weather was at our windows instead of being distant behind walls. Birds grouped for plunder and had to be obstructed by complicated entanglements of string and twists of paper. The cat hunted, quivering, in her forest, revealing a wickedness I had never imagined as she waited in the camouflage of her stillness under the wallflowers or wrapped round a tree branch. I watched her precision as she tortured the mice, her exact use of terror and physical violence to half-stun, half-incapacitate, and I suppressed the screams of a tension inside me that I could barely endure. Yet I watched, and dug my finger nails into my palms, and was a conspirator and a lover afterwards when I closed my hand over her white, fur breast and she hugged my wrist in silk and boneless paws.

Our neighbours' garden, even bigger but less excitingly stocked, ran L-shaped along two sides of ours, the privet thick and tall between us. And on the other side of that garden was a cinder-bottomed wilderness of quitch-grass and thistles at throat height, which had once had its brief glory as a private tennis court, was vaguely said to be the site of somebody's posh residence of the future, and whose vital importance was to be found in the high wooden fence which separated it from the recreation field – the Central Field or, as we knew it always, The Field.

That fence was the gateway to one third of my cultural life, the physically competitive part. Our garden ended on two of its sides at the walls of the tin chapel and the cinema, and they were the other two parts of my culture. They were supplemented, randomly, amusingly, often thrillingly, by books and the radio; but those three teachers – the arena, the theatre and the wailing wall – invaded and directed my being. All three were myth-makers and myth-breakers alternately, when I was hero, poet and saint, then coward, idiot and sinner. In all three I won understanding and suffered confusion. Being physically at the heart of them I was seldom free of their insistent pull or rejection, and they rattled my personality from one to another like dice.

The entry on to the Field had in itself a drama. I invariably went over the fence, which was at least a tall man's height on our side and so had to be climbed with a leap and a leverage, balls of the feet springing against the vertical, a twist and a roll of the body over the top. There was an eventfulness in that moment which never failed me. Beyond the fence were combat and brilliant moments and others of dread.

The grass sloped in a deep bulge on the other side, levelling to the flat of the football pitch. Over the months the field changed character, acquiring a concrete water tank away to the left, losing the clipped bowling green in the right-hand corner to wartime neglect and overgrowing tufts and weeds. But in the perfection in which I saw it first the field had white goalposts on a football pitch marked out in sawdust, the bowling green was a thick, green gleam, its pavilion was a cowboys' ranch-house in grey wood and corrugated iron, the air raid shelter was a great snail of red clay with brick at each end, and the plain ended far ahead and to the left in ditches and a frieze of stumpy trees and hawthorn berries. Behind the trees were the forbidden farm-lands owned and patrolled by the awful figure of Higgie, the coalman, with his face of thundercloud, his leggings and his lash. The fence ran on two sides only, securing green-houses and pigeon lofts from depredation.

The arena. The proving ground. The cockpit.

Its tradition as such was long. I already knew, although when I was told and by whom I could never pinpoint, because these things were the legends of the field, that grown men had fought each other to the brink of death here. The pictures were as clear in my head as if I had names and addresses for the men in them: the hurrying, noisy groups coming from the pub, through the big gates between the butcher's and the greengrocer's, the circle forming, and the vast chests and bare fists, and blood and shouts under a moon. There were more lurid nights than those, when the crowd's noise had the snarling and grinding of dogs in it: scarlet-eyed Staffordshire bull terriers with pig-pink bodies,

and one of them in the centre of the circle matched not
against another dog but against a man, brutish on his hands
and knees, streaked with red on his chest and his chin,
fighting with his teeth like the slavering dog.

'How long ago was that?'

'Last year.'

'It wor, yo liar. Doa yo believe 'im. My grandad doa
remember it.'

'Mine does. Ee sez it was every Saturday night.'

'Liar.'

'Well, they still make the dogs fight.'

'That ay the same. Dogs are meant to bite.'

'I bet our Red ud beat yourn.'

'We ay got a dog, yo daft bugger.'

'Our Red ud beat any dog.'

'I'll beat yo in a bit.'

In such headlong, impelled ways the challenges would be
made, the link with a savage, relished past sustained with an
unthinking ingenuity. Now the circle was real, although the
figures were smaller. Fists bunched tight and white beneath
their grime, the blood drained from under the fragile flesh
of the two staring faces, and two reputations collided bone
to bone, will to will, in a tearing of clothing, blinking of eyes,
nursing of ears, gurgling of fear. The damage was usually
trivial; submission was the defeat and the triumph. The prize
was domination.

We had our versions of the public school bullies, the
Flashmans and Gilkses of my reading: long trousers and
hair in greasy spikes, home-made catapults with stubby
forks and dangling rubber as long as braces. They smoked
dimps and hunted in threes and fours for victims to use for
improvised pleasures. The threats were terrifying:

'Let's 'ang 'im up on the tree by 'is belt.'

'Let's set fire to 'im.'

'I bet yo cor 'it 'im with yer catapult from the water tank.'

The victim ordered against the fence, crucifixion position, outguards cutting off any chance of escape: Flashman and Gilks standing close together, grinning, Gilks fitting a round stone into the leather joint of the heavy rubber.

'Doa yo move, kid. I'm gun 'it the fence by yer ear. Doa move.'

The catapult in position and the right hand yanking back towards the spittly grin: victim's eyes clenched tight, knees wobbling, stomach turned to icy sludge.

A sharp thud against the fence, a burst of laughter: eyes open to see the rubber ball bouncing back towards Flashman. And Gilks wanging the catapult at some darting sparrow.

One could survive against the gangsters; but that was the limit of any success against them. They ruled the Field, when they chose to give it their attention, with a sneering arrogance, sometimes setting up fights between a couple of small captives for their own casual amusement.

There were three alternative measures to be taken once they were sighted and their mood assessed as dangerous: run for home, which was hazardous because it was provocative and often involved an attempt to dodge past them; scatter for the cover of the corn beyond the ditch, and gamble that they wouldn't follow for fear of exciting Higgie into one of his rages; or tag on to them with a show of mute admiration, risking that such blatant cowardice would be held in contempt beyond interest and not be seized upon as willingness for slaughter. There were no romantic notions of little Davids vanquishing Goliaths. The challenge was to obstruct the vindictive will of power in circumstances where there was no institutional protection and which had no 'fair' and 'unfair'. There were the strong and the weak; the weak fled, hid or begged.

But numbers were important, and so was mood. These gangsters appeared to be harmless when alone, and there were times when together they were only languid and absorbed in their talk, to which we listened, privileged and ignored, sitting cross-legged in the tall grass, not properly understanding yet instructed in a vague way about the special thrill and uncertainty of their condition between ours and the adults':

'Our kid says they get you down and paint yer dick on the first day.'

'The blokes?'

'No, the wenches. They paint it black.'

'They doa, I bet. I cor see our Joan doin' that. 'Er works there.'

'It's right. Our kid sez so. First day at work the wenches paint yer dick.'

'Do all the blokes stand round?'

'I doa know. Our kid day say.'

'They doa do it at the pit.'

' 'Course they doa. There ay no wenches there.'

'Our kid sez they 'ad a wench's knickers off on the bus and 'ung 'em out the winder.'

'Do they paint the wenches' things an' all?'

'Naow. Our kid sez they 'ave 'em down in the storeroom in the dinner hour. Ee sez they pay the bloke.'

'They ought to paint the wenches an' all, I think.'

'Well they doa. Our kid sez. Any road, they ay got nothing to paint, 'ave they?'

They were Regency bucks in black plimsolls and their fathers' striped shirts baggy and flapping on their shoulders: lazy seekers of cruel diversions, conceited, lustful, semi-literate. They would wrestle each other, giggling and going for trouser buttons and shouting girls' names. But they could also be solemn on their way to the canal with fishing rods and tobacco tins with slugs in them, when they seemed aged and remote although they were still at school, if almost done with it. They did not fight with fists much. There was blood if they did, and some adult would appear and break up the circle.

But football engaged both age groups, and beyond. Real footballs were not common, and they were not always owned by the most obsessed players; nor was it at all certain that a football owner's mother would deliver up the ball if a deputation tried to borrow it. Reasons for refusal could be totally unsatisfactory:

'It's too wet.'

'I've never set eyes on yo before, or 'im with the red 'air.'

'If your mother can buy yo real football boots 'er can afford to buy yo a ball an' all.'

So when a football arrived at the field it was a presence that stopped all other activity. If a game was already being played with some other ball it was immediately abandoned. There was no exclusiveness; everybody played. We grouped on the bank behind one goal, ranging from eight-year-olds with curls like blossom to working youths with signet rings, and two captains would yell a name in turn, until only the frailest were left, and even they would be beckoned with a princely gesture:

'Yo can 'ave them two, Tom. Yo can use 'em as corner flags if yo like.'

There could be five or six on each team or more than twenty. The rules were followed in accordance with a deeper truth than the narrow detail of the letter, but never ignored: deliberate clutching at an opponent was a foul, and so was handling the ball; subtler nudgings and trippings worked into the flow of the action were accepted under our code, whose fundamental tenet was that effectiveness was legitimacy. A captain's contempt for the irrelevance of apologies could be withering:

'Eh, kid, doa waste time saying sorry every time yo trip somebody. Yo'm like a soft tart.'

Skill was abundant, and was never taught. Body swerves and feints and pouncing tackles came naturally from some of those lean figures like extensions of their mundane movements. The game animated the indolent and graced the gawky. It suspended classification of friend and enemy and replaced it with the judgement of good or bad player, and in changing the context of our relationships it revealed courage and invention and timidity where they had not been expected. Praise from some astonished adolescent, beaten for acceleration by a child four or five years younger, was immediately recognised for being either genuine or patronizing; and condescension was unacceptable in all this intensity:

'Never mind telling 'im 'ow good 'e is. Catch 'olt on 'im if yo cah play 'im. They'll bloody thrape us the way yo'm goin' on.'

The captains were not playing for fun. Their status was at stake:

'I woa pick yo again. Yo'm frit. Scared babby!'

The games would start around five in the evening, players turning up with slices of bread and jam like books in their fists. Only darkness stopped us.

There was a prize tantalizingly familiar in our talk and yet unattainably distant in our expectations. This was 'a Trial'. To be spotted by some passing stranger, or recommended by a local contact man with influence, and invited to the Wolves' ground for a trial match was the most desirable experience imaginable. We used the word casually – 'good enough for a trial', 'too small for a trial', 'too slow for a trial' – as if the event was a local common-place. In fact it was most unlikely then, because the war had

disrupted professional football. But the longing was in our
lore, along with the references. We judged each other's
chances daily and nightly; and daily and nightly we dreamed
of a personal, impossible triumph. Few of us at that stage
had ever seen Wolverhampton Wanderers' ground eight or
nine miles away by bus, but we used the names of Cullis and
Westcott and Galley like talismens:

'Stan Cullis!' The invocation would be hurled at the
advancing ball as the shouting defender crouched with his
elbows tensely hooked away from his sides, as if calling on
the name would add intimidation to his tackle.

'I'm Westcott!' The shout would strengthen the shot as
some four-foot-six centre-forward rushed on the goal behind
an inviting ground pass.

The goalposts were not permanent fixtures; the sawdust
lines on the pitch were infrequently renewed. Most of our
games were played with piles of jackets and pullovers for
goals, and we came to hard, grudging agreements on what
shots had gone over an imaginary crossbar. Football boots,
like footballs, were rare and were worn with swagger and
borrowed with awe. On holiday from school we would be
playing while the dew was still glinting in the grass before
the sun had cleared the chimney pots, and ploughing on
when the mud was at our laces and the leather ball was
weighted like a coal scuttle. Two players were enough to
make a game: star goal-keeper and penalty king.

'I won easy today.'

'You look as if you fell in the tar barrel.'

'Twenty-three seventeen, the score was. It's a record.'

'What for?'

'For me against 'im this week.'

The Central Cinema had an off-white front, big posters
in many-coloured paint and two show-cases of lusciously

seductive photographs. In those show-cases pinned still for savour were the exotics and the exquisites, the protectors and the menacers, the despicable and the flawless who were the prototypes for the stars in the casts of thousands whom I deployed in my tumultuous cinema of the mind.

I took these cowboy sheriffs, boy runaways, space pilots, singing sword-fighters, jungle lords, banjo comedians, minuscule Chinese detectives, coloratura goddesses, dimple-kneed flirts, blood-fed pirates, hero-dogs and men made of mud and I directed them in thunderous extravaganzas of the silver screen which stretched across the vastness of the inside of my forehead. I needed only seconds between one conscious activity and another to mount a galloping adventure of epic dimension. Poised between the tying of one shoelace and wrestling with the other, invincibly locked in some self-imposed knot overnight, I could summon cavalry by the column and glint at their head in a metallic charge at Geronimo's ochrous horde; could transmogrify while the dust still billowed and swing slab-thighed and bicepped like an elephant's leg on my rope of jungle creepers, and snatch some plane-wrecked blonde from the tentacles of a spider the size of a willow tree; and could still have time to change yet again, as I landed in the treetop with Blue Eyes fluttering in my armpit, into goggles and flying jacket and sweep onwards and upwards into lone battle in my spitting bi-plane cockpit against a skyful of Huns.

I was a hero with a hundred faces, all copies and composites of the idols in the showcases and yet on all of them was superimposed my own. For supporting players, rivals and heroines I mixed the famous with a brilliant audacity that no De Mille or Korda ever approached. Hoppalong Cassidy had his horse shot from under him by King Ming's bodyguard using ray guns; Shirley Temple got carried off by Zulu warriors; Mickey Rooney borrowed one of Tarzan's giraffes

for a race from the saloon to Boot Hill and back, got locked
in his room again for smoking and was replaced to triumphant effect by me. Usually, even if mechanized or airborne
at the moment of victory, I still rode out of my film on a tall,
piebald horse, waving my hat in the air, the adoring, grateful faces of all those figures in the showcase flickering
subliminally through the fade-out.

I knew the faces long before I saw them bloated in close-
up inside the cinema. Not all of them were regarded at home
as suitable for my interest. But they were already in my own
shows. I was a slinking private detective, on that precursor
of the Cinemascope screen that I carried behind my eyes,
before I had ever seen Bogart or Powell. I knew what dames
(hot) were, and rods ('You man enough to carry that thing,
Bud?'), and torpedos (out of town). Or at least I knew that
those thin-eyed, snappy hatted men in the striped suits used
those terms; the references were there in the captions under
the showcase pictures. Imagination was enough to turn
those pictures into a wealth of stories, tricky with sudden
turns of fate, reckless with fists and gunfire. The showcase
pictures changed every three days, but it was not often
enough to match my impatience for new faces, new circumstances.

To begin with I got inside the building only on Saturday
afternoons. It was a simple hall with one floor of tip-up
seats. There was one price, which for a long time was four-
pence (and I think I remember its being twopence), and we
were divided roughly into smallest at the front, biggest at
the back. We chattered like a football crowd on the radio.
Mr Bates, the proprietor, yelled for order and did not get it
until he produced one of his celebrated crescendos which
brought bits of plaster showering from the ceiling and were
known to still the rooks in the trees across the recreation
field:

'WILL YOU BE QUIERRRRRT. . . .'

A hush like the Armistice Day silence would fall, but it would not last as long.

While the sixguns were blazing, the Indians whooping, the fists battering, the space-ships plunging to doom, we were as good as gold. But we regarded conversation on the screen as the most tedious inactivity, to be filled in by re-enacting the last fight or by throwing whatever rubbish could be found about the floor or in our pockets at faces currently in disfavour. The noise would rise to a point of zoo-like bedlam, until Mr Bates's voice would again soar above it and beat it into submission:

'. . . . . WORRRRRNIN' YOOOO . . . . . ALL OUT . . . LAST CHANCE.'

We would subside, explode again. Deanna Durbin would be silenced in mid trill and her frilly presence replaced by the shiny-shoed, black-jowled one of Mr Bates, who would point out a few ringleaders to be plucked from their seats by his assistant and hustled up the gangway and out into the daylight. We would yawn through the solemn, bawling lecture that followed, Deanna would be restored to the cloud, high on which she had been waltzing, waltzing, and we would sit out the rest of the gooey goings-on in a muttering agony of boredom until she vanished in a smile of petticoats and we could sink our eyeballs into the unflagging action of the Johnny Mack Brown or Flash Gordon serial with which Mr Bates, patient, decent, sensible businessman that he was, invariably sent us home. At Christmas he stood at the door as we left and gave each of us apples and oranges. His normal speaking voice was a ruin; and we, no doubt, were the wreckers.

But I laid siege to the adults' cinema of the night, tire-lessly nibbling away at denial by means of whine, wheedle, sweetness and logic, until the principle was established: I could go to the pictures in the evening, first house, show commencing at 5.30, on my own. To begin with there was always an interrogation from my mother about what the film was called and who was in it, although since my parents never went to the cinema she clearly had to work literally by ear. If the title sounded 'too old', violent or salacious my case was heavily prejudiced against me before a word of argument was spoken:

'What's on?'

'Jerrmerrn.'

'What?'

'G-men.'

'No.'

'It's only a detective.'

'No.'

'Granville's seen it. He says it's tame.'

'No.'

'Everybody's seen it but me.'

'No.'

'I've finished my library books.'

'No.'

'Granville says it's ever so slow.'

'No.'

'Well Thursday, Friday and Saturday it's only a love film.'

There was a calculated risk in a piece of pleading like that last one. 'Love film' sounded unsuitable, I knew, but if I disparaged it in advance it would suggest that I would not be putting up a claim for going to the pictures in the second half of the week, for which mercy a concession might be made in the case of the disputed 'detective'. On the other hand the duty of parental censorship might override the bargaining convention, so that I was in danger of drawing a blank week. Such disaster did not strike often. Adroitly Mr

Bates usually managed to balance three days of tommy guns and beating up in Chicago with three of ballad singing in Maytime or clean family living in Massachusetts.

I did not very much care, except when it came to cowboys or costume swashbuckle (pirates, Spanish galleons, the thin red line against the savages), about the subject matter; I was drawn by the aura, the event, the surprise, the mystery. The appeal was aesthetic in a markedly austere way, because the Central Cinema was as bare as a bus; there was nothing in the environment here to cosset the body, and I was too young for the back rows and the hugs and fumbling. Yet the place excited all my senses, not just my curiosity. On my own in the dark and yet not laughing or wincing alone, puzzled and embarrassed by my secret tears, alerted in the guts, morally offended, dizzy with giggles, I recognized technique, the significance of close-ups and dissolves in emphasizing aspects of character and plot, in a way that did not apply when I was reading books. To recognise this technique was like mastering some new craft; it was an essentially private accomplishment, not at all like learning the meaning of unfamiliar words, which could be entertaining but was all the same a public duty, like knowing who found Moses in the bullrushes. I liked *films*, not just particular ones, now that I could go to the pictures at night.

The official gradings of 'A' and 'U', which were supposed to decide whether people like me could enter a cinema without an accompanying adult, were observed with a commercial interpretation at the Central Cinema, untainted by any psycho-moral complications. First house, being the more thinly attended, was the one we were welcome at, 'A' or 'U', except when the film was so popular that it attracted big queues. Then, as when one of us lost concentration when inside the cinema and became troublesome, the 'A' clause was invoked by the management who combed out the minnows as if our impudence had never been heard of before.

So I assimilated a great deal of material, doubtlessly of low artistic quality, which was invaluably educative. I learned, for example, something of the relationship between husband and wife that had never occurred to me in the unthinking observation of my parents; there was a 'love' interest between such people, for one thing (mildly expressed, since this was long before the days of the explicit, hand-up-the-mini-skirt film); their partnership could be threatened by a third party, for another. There were certainly long passages of these nights when, jammed on one dead buttock against an arm rest, my neck stretching to see the screen between the two shoulder pads in front, I understood nothing at all of the action; when accusations and intrigue were as impenetrable as if they were spoken in Urdu. But I accepted my ignorance without resentment, gripped by the movement, by the expectation that at any moment the story would jolt alive again into a blaze of anger, a twist of cruelty, a glistening of heroism. I was frequently frightened, when I thought I might pee in my terror, but would shut my eyes for only a second and was immediately ashamed. There were moments when I felt golden all over with the brilliance of my understanding.

The cinema's black cat sometimes walked with infinite self-absorption across the foot of the screen, delivering its shadow into the gaping mouth of some dying cowboy or between the breasts of some Eastern temptress with her fingers in the grapes, and the spell would break, the place would bray with derisive laughter. Or the screen would shimmer in a momentary palsy, jabber and be dead, and the lights would go on to a coughing of disgust and a satisfying sigh over other people's incompetence. The interruptions were a proper part of the event, of the aura. It was not the slickness in the films that made this place so magnetic, so entrancing; it was rich with the unexpected, not least in our responses. It traded irresistably in the pleasures of vulgarity.

'Can I go to the pictures tonight?'

'What's on?'

'Skaafis.'

'What?'

'Scarface.'

'No.'

'It isn't *all* shooting.'

'No.'

'Granville says it's nearly as slow as an English film.'

'No.'

'I think I'll mow the lawn tomorrow night.'

'You're not going.'

'It's only some love film Thursday, Friday and Saturday. . . . . .'

God directed us to the tin chapel, although the name he used for it was The Mission. He appointed my father to the task of reviving its defunct Sunday School and to an imprecise, all-embracing duty as unpaid choirmaster, youth club leader, door repairer, baby christener, keeper of the keys and district spiritual guide. The rest of the family supported him as our talents permitted in counting pennies, pouring tea, dusting seats, singing solos and being good.

Sunday had always had ceremony, with glinting shoes and fresh white collars, fluffy muffs on rich girls' laps, handshaking in the chapel porch and solemn anthems reeling with Amens in a smell of damp dust and grannies' breath. All that had been in the big, lead-windowed church half an hour's walk away in the town. It was the smart church, where the shop owners' wives wore fur coats and their children burrowed icy-tipped noses into them like piglets

going for teats; where ponderous men, hung with watch-
chains like girt horses, bore collecting plates down the
aisles in a trance of piety. There a man played an organ with
pipes like half a forest of elms, and on a grave-cold, blackout night, when the pavements had shattered stars on them,
I had felt a thin knife drawn clean through my head from
ear to ear as a tiny woman with a round white face (she had
come specially from London, I was told) sang I Know That
My Redeemer Liveth, and held me skewered and chilled
rigid among the warm breathing of the worsted around me.
There old preachers told relentless stories about sons'
neglect of white-haired fathers in a tedious section of the
morning service called Children's Address; and other old
men, booted and guttural, jerked out of slumber to shout
'Preach-the-gospel' at young preachers, and were shushed at
and blushed at by squirrel-ruffed daughters with robins'
beaks. There I sang my first public performance, in a white
satin shirt, standing out alone while the rest of the choir sat,
and was terrified and important, and amazed by my own
perfection, and my brother had his bike pinched from the
vestry.

From that big place we sometimes returned home with
the prize of the visiting minister, and sat him with reverence
in my father's chair, poured him water in the one crystal
glass which had survived the myriad removal men and
watched every shred of cabbage and roast beef into his
mouth as if he was a saintly unicorn entrusted to our feeding.
The big place was called Trinity, and God had chosen us
from its congregation to convert the heathen and the
drunkards' children of Blackfords.

The tin chapel was lined inside with brown and cream
wood, blistered near the railed stove and glistening with
condensation in the corners. It had a pedal organ and a
pulpit, but no choir stall. It had movable wooden benches,

known as forms, and a little kitchen at the back smelling severely of leaking gas, where vast brown teapots and piles of cups and plates packed the cupboards.

This wealth of domestic equipment, together with the benches and some trestle tables, comprised the tin chapel's most-valued service to the community. It furnished wedding receptions and 21st birthday parties, Christmas bun feasts at the working men's clubs, funeral teas and old folks' treats. It was borne away on handcarts and in women's pillow-like arms to the vexed tut-tutting of the chapel-goers, not at all sure that the Lord would ever forgive the beer stains on the wood or the belching profanities that were known to breathe over the crockery.

These chapel-goers were mostly women, a small group of squat, varicose, cracked-fingered martyrs to drudgery and powerlessness. Collectively their main characteristics were black clothing and a contralto wail. They were at their saddest, and their most content, when they gathered on mid-week afternoons for their mothers' meeting, weary and graceless as they greeted each other in gloom at the gate, shuffling with a hacking of death rattles across the floor and moaning through their relished hymns of entreaty and despair:

'What a friend we have in Jesus, All our sins and griefs to bear.'

'I am trusting Thee, Lord Jesus, Trusting only Thee.'

'O love that wilt not let me go, I rest my weary soul in Thee.'

'Abide with me, Fast falls the eventide.'

The voices rose in a ragged pleading and drifted in the air – a cloud of crows' throats bleeding into our chimney pots. The women supplicated with a deliberate, practised misery, finding a pleasure in joylessness, showing their scars to a world they would never forgive. Whatever optimism had ever flickered in their lives had long ago vanished in the habit of fear and its balm, self-pity. These miners' wives and mothers and widows were the extreme product of their environment, just as the cripples of the pit were:

'Help of the helpless, O abide with me.'

My father lit this glum place with children. They crowded in on Sunday afternoons with starlings' density and chatter, whole families of them filing in linked by hands held behind and in front like a march of baby elephants, marvel-eyed under toddlers' lamb-curls and hulk-shouldered in mothers' best coats. There were boys with donkeys' voices and girls with smokers'. There were girls with feet of stone and boys with velvet ears. There were boys with smells of rabbit hutches and girls like a fire at the soap works. We were crammed on the benches, skin to skin, breath to breath, our ankles hooked like wickerwork. We each seemed to have five knees. We had moments of sanctity, as when reading aloud of Benjamin or Esau or the afflictions of the righteous, and getting every syllable right; and we had pangs of utter evil-doing when we sniggered over the fit of our forefingers in our belly buttons during prayers and my father's silence was an archangel's rebuke. Out of that silence we could hear as plain as twigs on a window-pane the scratch of the pen as God, a billion miles away at his desk beyond the moon, wrote our names in his big black book. And we sang.

Singing was our true function. I knew that – had always known it – because I could transform the whole world's climate of opinion by the use of my limber treble. A rendering of Once-in-Royal-David's, or Once-A-Boy-a-Wild Rose, or Oh-For-the-Wings, I had long ago observed, sent over-talkative aunts into a grinning daze, snuffed out parental reproach, evaporated domestic tension of every kind. I sang to bribe, to disarm, to apologize, to confound, to reward, and quite often for personal pleasure. I enjoyed the talent for its own sake, because my expertise with tunes was clearly uncommon. I was not to know that it was really meagre and would soon be removed from me by a treachery of my own body, to be replaced not by an equally smooth adult version but by a blunt baritone of striking uncertainty. At the moment it was a busy skill, providing status and at times a considerable emotional ripple; the Methodists' hymns can be plaintive, muscular and moving in simplicity as well as creepy in melancholy.

When grouped in our crush of ambiguous sopranos most Sundays of the year we were a matter of bold good will more than a musical event. But on one Sunday every summer, a day when the boys blushed for the compromising prettiness of the roses on our lapels and the girls glistened in their brittle satinette like spools of tinsel, we were a heavenly host. This was The Anniversary, when a choir of the chosen, trained to impeccability by my father's patience, was raised on a specially built platform, tangy with moist wood, and performed to packed houses morning, afternoon and evening. We had special, acrobatic tunes with shrieking choruses among the familiar hymns, and once a girl called Daisie with limbs made of glass sang some devout verses to the tune of *Danny Boy*, shocking the pious ladies in their hats of orange peel. (Anniversaries were common to all the chapels of the district, and were visited in turn by the garden-wall critics, as if doing the season at Salzburg.) I, of course, had solos as well, trembling in my new socks but sufficiently in control to decide in mid-performance whether I was being as good as Webster Booth this time or merely the best boy singer alive. Afterwards we discussed the quality of the show:

'You was crooking yer 'ead on the side agin.'
'Wasn't.'
'Was.'
'Wozitgorradoowiyou?'
'Yeah, see.'

'Wasn't.'

'Was. Any road, you was flat.'

'Liar.'

'Yeah, see.'

'Wasn't.'

'Was.'

We went to other people's Anniversaries and sneered. We had nothing to do with religion then. Once we were in sight of the tiered platform we were showbiz, jealous and two-faced and afraid for our reputations. Sweet indeed was the work, my God, my King, to praise Thy name, give thanks and sing, but it was altogether sweeter to be assured on all sides that they couldn't hold a candle to us up at Bethel or at Salem, where that snooty Buckley woman, 'er that scraped on the violin like next door's cats, was throwing 'er weight about.

The religious teaching of the tin chapel, and of the rest of the pulpits on this intensely competitive circuit, was assimilated as a jumble of cautionary tales of the errors of the spirit, never specified, and some doubtful advice for the young about deportment in the face of provocation:

'Now then, suppose you're going for a walk after,' one of my father's helpers was telling a little group of us, 'and you meet another gang that wants to fight. Right, now 'ow can yo get out of it? What would the disciples 'ave done? You could say, "Eh, no, I can't, I've got mi best clowthes on." Or you could say, "It teks two to mek a fight, and I'm not fightin' on a Sunday." '

This was, I suppose, a brave attempt at bringing Christian doctrine down to practical relevance. We gawped, and said Yes and No and turned to secret contests in holding our breath. We were not much excited by Jesus, with that night shirt on and the lamp in his hand. He was right, of course; not about anything in particular, just Right. It made him boring.

Yet the reiterated affirmations and the warnings from the wagging finger penetrated and adhered. God undoubtedly Was, and it was improper to ask was What? He watched and noted and placed us all first this side and then that of the dividing line between nice and nasty. Our names flitted in and out of that list he kept of those to be invited to the permanent cream-cake-and-tea-with-condensed-milk party which constituted life after death for the ones who washed their necks and kept their wet shoes off the bench in front.

Between the perpetual mourning of the camphorated old women and the boisterous jocularity directed at us by other religious adults we absorbed some kind of faith, a habit of acceptance of some logical, adjudicating, wrong-righting authority beyond the eye and the fist of visible, tangible people. We had a mixture of unease and smugness. The old women were a glowering, misanthropic bunch, repeating over and over that they were rough diamonds whose reward would be in heaven; it would all come out in the wash; blessed were the poor; suffer the little children; Jesus loved me; what a friend we had in Jesus.

But he wouldn't let me play football on Sundays. I was lucky, or specially favoured; there were some kids, I heard, whom he wouldn't allow to *run* on the Sabbath, not even to Sunday school.

4

Some Characters

Granville was one of those children who, because of the magic quality of their childishness, remain unimaginable as adults. If I recall to my mind the looks, the attitudes, the natures of the children I was a child with I can visualize nearly all of them quickly enough as grown up: the thin, sniffy, sour-tempered ones now six feet tall and nicotined and grumbling about the year-by-year diminishing of the number of matches in a new box; thick-nosed Fred must now be podgy all over in industrial grey, florid and burpy with his carload of Fredlets fed on potato crisps and cheez-o-bix; dark-eyed Walter with the elegant stance must now be the handsome philanderer of some housing estate, with a Cleopatra of a wife and his blue-black hair sleek as a labrador's; one of the Johns, the one who began early drifting off with girls, will now be a henpecked drinker getting ever closer to the murder of the one he had to marry. But Granville is still ten, with a yellow face like a grinning sun on a bucket-and-spade travel poster, plump legs and arms with no evident bones and a mind of marvellous invention, utterly incorruptible by confrontation with fact or by the threats of authority. He was without fear of mystery; a poet, who never saw mundanity.

He lived in a brooding, silent house with his mother, who was seldom seen, and with the overriding, elusive presence of his father, permanently absent and engaged in a bewildering variety of heroic and saintly deeds abroad in the war. There he was by turn every manner of fighting man from pilot to white Ghurka, and also both a doctor, hacking off gangrenous limbs with natives' knives, and a padre, quelling the terrors of the shell-shocked with his silver-tongued prayers and his miraculous show of indestructibility as he strode alone among the bullets in the brilliant light of the moon.

Granville's father was to me one of the great figures of the world's fiction, and for years I had to make considerable effort to rid myself of surprise that he was not more widely known, along with Rockfist Rogan and Sir Lancelot and Sidney Carton. He won medals by the week, could speak a dozen languages, was a personal friend of General Montgomery, had relieved an Italian field marshal of a crateful of cigars now to be delivered to Mr Churchill, and was to become a composer the moment he got home. The conviction, the detail, the fluency of these assertions and circumstantial accounts made them too compelling to be disregarded. Granville had the true artist's gift: he showed us truth where we scoffed there was none.

His absent father was Superdad. In Granville's longing comicalities I saw a hero who could survive a thousand exposures of lies. We dismissed him with pedantry, and Granville resurrected him with glory. Only his physical return could have destroyed him, and I never saw that, not because it did not occur but because by then Granville and I were separated by the gulf that stretched between two different schools.

When Granville was not boasting of his incomparable father he was manufacturing magnificent dramas of battle in which he and I crushed armies of the world's villainry, from apes to Japs. These encounters were different from my own filmic triumphs in that they were physical, aloud and engendered sweat, and not wide-awake dreams of solo

conquest. We raged about his long garden, cantering through
the trees of rhubarb, squirming along the potato trenches,
chat-chatting with our throaty machine-guns, always allies
against the Axis. He thought for us both, a guerrilla leader of
brilliant improvisation or a battle commander of massive
ruthlessness. We flattened half a nation of soldiers with our
bombardment of mud-bombs, and we bayonetted the strag-
glers to horrible deaths against the clothes-line post. We
never fought each other.

Granville brought to all this violence a passion that
possessed us both. In that drab, sopping garden behind the
tall fence we fought his father's war and killed everyone in
sight who could not speak English. It was a private world
with us. We never took our artillery to my own garden, or
into the street. But once Granville was persuaded to bear his
collection of toy pistols, rifles and shotguns to some other
place, to be distributed among a group of our friends, so
that two teams could be formed for a more realistic battle.
The occasion was limp, the collective wit too dull, the
integrity absent. The guns soon dropped in the grass, and
the two armies fraternized and deserted. Granville was like
an exhausted Zapata or Garibaldi or Guevara, dispirited by
the presence of mercenaries, the inquisitive, cynical ones
without commitment. He sulked, and the unbelievers sneered
that it was kids' stuff and left in derision. He gathered his
arsenal, the buttery face slack and pouched, and began the
retreat. His feet dragged. I let him go alone.

His attitude to classroom work had the same startling,
urgent ingenuity as his games. He was incapable of thought
in the disciplined, utilitarian way. The logic of arithmetic
and the order of syntax were matters of agonizing tedium to
him, and his guileless poet-idiot's responses brought him
gales of laughter and the stick.

Three times seventeen? 'It's like a bird, Miss.' What,

what, what? 'When you chalk, Miss, doing three, Miss.'
Laughter and swish and no more nonsense.

He had a vision of a winter which was a delicious Never-
Never time: a glassy-white, silver-peopled, fogless, cloud-
less, coughless time in which children were the effortless
skaters and all the adults fell down and broke their legs.

He was the voice of childhood, uninhibited, incorrigible
and doomed. When the printed word was beyond him he
spotted the reason and yelled it out to us without hesitation.
'It's all in Latin and French, Miss.' Laughter and swish and
no more nonsense.

Only other children could hurt him, because he expected
malevolence from adults. A little group, with colder intelligence than he had, discussed his capacity for make-believe,
and for believing it, and decided to turn it against him: to
make use of what he loved most and show its betrayal to
him. It was a vicious, clever trick. They hinted, then
refused to confirm, the existence of a secret tunnel which
stretched from under the back yard of the terrace of houses
where they lived to its emergence in some imprecise spot, as
yet not established, on the other side of the road, perhaps in
the field beyond his garden. The bait was irresistible. He
persisted; they shrugged, denied, relented, invited him to
the meeting place, behind the lavatories in their communal
yard. He saw, just in time as he got near, the hot coke of evil
in their eyes, and turned and ran for his life, while they
chased and screamed with their fists bunched.

'They were gunna do me,' he said to me later. 'You *knew*.'

He was lost. The world, *his* world of children, was incomprehensible to him.

'Only a game,' I said. 'A tunnel's kids' stuff. They didn't
pretend to *me*.'

He stared and thought, and did not find an answer.

* * *

Albert's mother was the fattest woman in the world. She would have been on show in a tent at Skegness, so we gave each other to understand, if there hadn't been a war on. Together with the great girth went every conceivable appendage that could draw attention to it. Around the vast breasts, like hundredweight bags of McDougall's Self-Raising, clung always a greeny-black material of shine and shadow which wobbled and quivered like mud under clear water as she breathed; and hanging loose from those buttress shoulders, just short of the billowing backside, was a cardigan of heavy wool that would have provided socks for half our Air Force; and projecting outwards from the improbable waist was an arrangement of old sacks to serve as aprons, stiff and steaming as if on an over-galloped horse; and issuing from the depths of all this flesh and fabric there came the voice of a pride of Tarzans.

It was a sound to engulf the village. When Albert's mother opened her mouth every dog and chicken and hollyhock braced itself for the shock waves. In affection, anger or defence, she used her capacity for noise as her special expression of proprietorship, as if by drowning her house, furniture, garden, husband, son, with her voice she was drinking them down into that great bosom, to be trapped in a blubbery fastness.

'Alberrrt . . . I'll cut yer arse off!'

The telegraph wires thrummed at the impact, cats hunched and shrivelled to mice, the milkgirl's little horse crossed himself with his tongue and ate his ears in a gulp. Albert, late again for some vital duty like fetching the bread or carrying the hens' feed, froze into a column of putty before our eyes, then disintegrated in a series of flicks and twitches from top to bottom, jerked instantly together again and pelted for home with wasps up his trousers.

It was never known to the rest of us whether Albert's

mother ever converted these awful threats into physical effect. Albert was in a permanent state of electrification because of what his mam would do to him; but he never reported what she *had* done. A woman of such a presence, and with such a visitation as that voice at her command, would hardly need the trivial recourse of corporal violence. It must have been like sharing a house with some animate, excitable Queen of Bells, an implacable Great Dong who had to be treated with the most servile attentiveness, lest the slightest offence should set up a vibration which would send the creature waddling into an intolerable din.

Albert was a cut-down version of his father, thin and long and sallow-enamel, the two of them bowed at the shoulders and with a meek wariness in their eyes. I went occasionally into Albert's house, afraid, my head crammed into goose-pimples as if into a thimble, and was always impressed by the depth of the silences which followed his mother's detonations. It did not matter if she was smiling or frowning, if she was referring to weather or ration books or one of Albert's recent sins: her volume overwhelmed, as if it gobbled up all the oxygen in the air and left us sagging and incapable of response. When Albert's mother laughed her husband and son would commiserate in glances at each other, holding on to chair arms and table tops until the floor settled back to level again.

There was an extraordinary, surreal occurrence at Albert's house one evening; or, to be exact about it, in his chicken pen. We found ourselves there, Albert and a John and a Tom and Tom's little brother and me, in the same bemused way that we would sometimes set off to go bilberry picking and suddenly discover, hours afterwards, that we were still sitting against somebody's back steps drugged on raw carrots stolen ice-cold and betel-potent from the earth. Similarly surprised and uncaring, there we were dawdling up the entry to Albert's garden with a number of unmatched boxing gloves of different sizes and lopsided conditions dangling in our hands.

There were no chickens in Albert's chicken pen, for reasons since obscured. Its square shape, sandy-sawdusty surface and surrounding wire mesh made it a natural boxing ring. We began a tournament, permuting name with name, allowing the handicap of one-arm-behind-the-back for biggest against smallest, claiming temporary identities with Len Harvey, Larry Gains, Joe Louis, Tommy Farr and, most clamorously, peerless Rockfist Rogan. Off we went, to a bang on the dustbin lid, the gloves variously like cabbages and old carpet slippers on our fists, jabbing and ducking, shoulders nudging knowingly under our chins. Len Harvey had just taken a wicked bit of body punching from Tommy Farr, when Albert's mother exploded upon the scene.

'Thrape 'im, Tommy. Go on, Tom-tom. Heeeeeh-he-he-heeeeh.'

The effect of this sound, and of the sight of that double-water-butt chest lurching at us, was if as we had been instantly transported to some enormous, rearing, bloodshot audience. She was a vivid cymbal banging in our heads, obliterating every other awareness, urging on our fists far beyond the careful mimicry of our play.

'Heeeeeh-he-he-heeeeh. Uppercut, Tommy!'

The frantic nature of the punching, headlong and oblivious on the impetus of this deafening driving force, was such that few blows actually struck flesh. We stared at each other between flurries, streaked red and white with effort, in no animosity but in a daze of competitiveness, while Albert's mother screeched and clapped her hands in what was plainly a condition of unblemished joy. We were like circus dogs with some outrageous Madame Fru-Fru gone mad with power.

But there was greater grotesquerie to come. Albert's mother, giggling like the butcher's pig-shed on slaughtering night, and her every bevelled corner shaking in conflicting rhythms, entered the chicken pen and announced she would take on all-comers. She put on two of the ragged gloves, a couple of fingers overflowing from each, and careered in great howling, sweating, tallow-fleshed stampings among us. We punched back in mindless duty. She was a tottering hall-stand hung with bolsters, and yet she went clang-clang.

The sun went down on this amazing event, and with the arrival of a damp dusk came a subduing of fever, a successive diminution of squawks and gasps and giggles, and at last she shook the gloves from her hands with one final great shimmy, shrieked 'Alberrrt!' and went slurp-pershlop through the kitchen door.

We looked at each other, blinking our way back from delirium, said nothing and drifted separately home.

When I got there I announced that I'd been boxing with Albert's mother, and they said 'Oh yes, hmmm,' in an equable, dismissive way, as if such an episode was commonplace.

We were joined sometimes by a sad, uncommon figure of rickety assembly and haphazard speech, called Vic. His age was indeterminable, and a subject of recurrent speculation. He was a kind of village indulgence or communal responsibility. He was special because it was impossible to categorize him except as himself.

He was not lunatic, although he could barely read or count or frame a dozen consecutive words to make a spoken sentence. He was not a cripple in the sense of immobility, although he could not co-ordinate the movements of his limbs with enough certainty to go to work. He was seen in public houses, so was not a child; but he kept school hours

in the daytime, emerging from his house when we were free
for play, and out and about all day long when we were on
holiday. He was treated as a child by children and as an
adult by adults. He was ugly and disjointed and he stam-
mered and spat; yet there was quickly recognisable in him
an intention of gentleness struggling to work its way
through the brutish surface and the built-in tangle of
communication equipment that frustrated him. This tenderness was visible in his face, which would lose its twist and
let the helplessness in the eyes make the point when the
tongue could not overcome its knots. He looked more of a
man, more deserving of civility then than at any other time.
Not even the most pampered, most timid of the local
children was ever frightened by poor, preposterous Vic.

His passion for football brought him dramatic, alarming
collisions. He would come lurching and capering into our
games, knees collapsing and scissoring beyond management,
elbows flicking and fingers jerking up and down, left and
right, as he fought in his own way to maintain a precarious
verticality with the ground. 'I's in g-g-goal,' he would shout,
heading for the place of glamour where he could imagine
his possession of easy agility and faultless timing. This was
very touching: the tortured angularity, the blundering
dizzy movements, the face clamped in earnestness, and his
bellowing monosyllables of rage and frustration as he missed
the ball and crashed in a heap in the mud. He made a noise
like a spilled box of dominoes when the ground was hard.
But he would struggle upright, spitting and gurgling,
teetering backwards on his heels, thrusting his long white
jaw up in front and his long cheese-wire fingers down behind
in another of his unique acts of balance. Someone hit him
hard in the face from close in on one occasion, when we had
a real football with a leather casing and an inexpertly tied
leather lace sealing the aperture. The lace bit into his skin,

slashing one of his eyebrows, and there was a spurt of blood. We hesitated. 'S-s-s'all right,' he shouted, brushing the blood away with a thumb and bringing another little gush; and he aimed a kick at the ball, missed, spun round twice in a flailing of arms as if overbalancing in a rowing boat, and settled in an absurd imitation of a goal-keeper's crouch, the thin head wagging and shaking spots of blood on to his knees. He looked heroic.

He was totally inept at football. His unpredictable movements influenced the game in a furious lucky-dip way; the ball struck him often. If he managed to catch it in both hands that tautly misshapen face would relax into a little boy's beam of wonder. If he socked the ball with his fist he would hee-haw in triumph.

There were times when his incapacities were misread by people not familiar with him; when someone would make a hasty assumption of imbecility or abjection and, trying to impress the rest of us, would play the tormentor. I watched one of these incidents with a rancid fascination. The interloper was red-haired and tubby and he had a sprig of elder which he kept jabbing into Vic's face, tickling and yapping. Vic made his clumsy brushing-away movements with his hands, struggling to speak, the splayed fingers missing the twig and scraping his nose and chin, and the red-haired boy laughed in delight at this bonus. Vic's face screwed up into a look of deepest bewilderment, and then abruptly changed into the normal features of an irritated adult, as his emotions overpowered his physical and nervous defects and blazed a path through the shame and humility which usually obscured other feelings. He stumbled forward, threw out those rusty-hinged arms and clasped them shut, and the red-haired boy found himself in a metallic, rattling embrace, which must have felt like being held between two rows of clucking false teeth. Vic was mouthing some unintelligible imprecations:

'I's g-g-gun-gun-gunna-ger-gun-gun. . . .' The red-haired
boy was squealing and sobbing in terror.

We watched callously. Vic squeezed those sharp-edged
arms, his wrists crossed and his hands going like a pair of
pecking birds. When he unravelled himself, stumbling and
still keeping hold of his captive for balance, first with one
hand and then with the other, he was gasping from his
stomach. The red-haired boy, released at last, was white and
blank in the face like a pudding cloth across a basin. Then
great sobs welled up from round his braces and came bubb-
ling through his lips, and he went back home with a dis-
graceful secret to hide about the day he went bear-baiting
and the beast broke loose.

But poor Vic was broken by a trickier, deeper-plunging
intrusion into his grievous privacy. My group heard about
it in troubling, piecemeal snatches; overheard about it, more
accurately. Some working youths, turning idleness into
elaborate cunning, pondered on his sexual interest and
capability and decided to try him out. That Beryl, they said
to him, the tall one with the glasses and the red nose, she
was sweet on him; she was easy, as well, they told him. He
was a man, wasn't he? She was eating her heart out for him,
they said; but he'd have to push himself a bit. Go on, Vic,
they told him. Why didn't he wait in the entry for her? When
it got dark? She went for fish and chips on Thursdays, half-
past eight about. He was a man, wasn't he?

So it seems that Vic took up his position in the gloom of
the entry halfway along the terrace row, with a collar on
and a tie in a knot like a prune-stone under his left ear, and
his boots polished. And the gaunt Beryl came clattering
down the gully in her wedge-soled shoes, was suddenly set
upon by this jabbering, shuffling rapist smelling of coal-shed
and dog-lust, and she screamed and hit out, and Vic grabbed
and gabbled, and they fell down, and Vic's trouser buttons

were undone as always, and the watching youths ran off as people arrived and sent for the policeman.

'Well, I knew summat like that ud 'appen woon o' these nights,' old women said in the bread queue.

'Yo cor trust 'em, these dafties.'

'They should put 'im away soomwheer.'

'It's the devil rising-gup in 'im, Missis.'

Vic was not put away, but he had to go to court, where Beryl told her story of outrage and the policeman explained how hard it was to gather a coherent explanation from the defendant, but that he appeared to be implicating some other persons who were not present.

Vic returned to us, morose and enfeebled. He sat on the bank like a dead bonfire and watched us play football, but he never went in goal again.

The first piano teacher who tried to summon and shape the musical genius in my sister and me was a young man of extreme fragility, with a skin made of spiders' webs and a manner of permanent, apologetic exhaustion. He came to our house sunk in a dark overcoat which increased his fugitive look, and sat beside us as we zigzagged through our scales with the attitude of a man glad to be enjoying the rest. We did not have him long. He taught us an elementary musical grammar – upon which we never built, for reasons which will shortly be given – showed us that music could be funny (an invaluable, rare lesson, as I have since observed, and one for which I have been grateful), began coughing and turning yellow one afternoon in the middle of a piece we had named Sugar Pig, and went shakily away to his bed, not to return.

After him we had the bolt-upright, come-down-in-the-world Mrs Pearson with letters after her name on a card in her front window.

We went to Mrs Pearson's house; she did not come to ours. (I never knew whether the fragile young man had a house; I had a vague picture in my mind of his nightly return to some kind of hospital where he and numerous others like him wheezed through sleep in metronomic unison.) Mrs Pearson's house, she told us often, was not at all the sort of thing she was used to. *He*, that is her husband, had brought her to these lower waters by permitting himself to grow old and then retire from his important position as a manager of some sort at the gas-works. The consequent reduction in income had meant that they had been forced to give up their bee-yoo-tiful home at some place which sounded like Cake Icing and reside in this terrace house without a hall and with the toilet across the yard. What was more Mrs Pearson had been forced to resume her profession as a music teacher, after several years in retirement, in order to maintain her table and her children in the highly superior condition to which she was accustomed. She was, as no doubt we had already noticed, many years younger than *him*, and she would never for one moment suggest that she minded all this extra work but she did only have one pair of hands, and they had to be looked after for professional reasons, and sometimes it really didn't seem as if people fully appreciated what a wrench it had been to leave her bee-yoo-tiful home, which was ever so private, and come to this row which really was not what she was used to at all. Mrs Pearson could produce an impressive sigh, for such a moulted little feather-duster of a woman with a throat like a thumb.

Her front room was heavy with dangling table cloths and sideboard cloths and chair covers in sombre greens and browns, and in summer and winter a deep fire, soused by a mound of wet slack, growled and hissed and brooded in the black grate. The net curtains were chinkless against the outside world; the room was as dim as a wardrobe. Mr and Mrs Pearson's different triumphs were set up on the walls: certificates with curly lettering in gilt frames for her precision at the keyboard and his longevity and devotion in the care of gas pipes. He had a presentation gold watch as well; her *real* reward, of course, was to impart her ability to others, she emphasized, although she thought she had fulfilled her vocational responsibilities a long time ago.

We went to her separately. I would falter through whatever little task she had selected for home-practice the week before, and she would call out the overlooked or misread notes as I skidded wide of them, her little voice sharp as a catbite. But once that chore was quickly out of the way she would turn her attention, and mine, to the principal function of the half-hour, which was for her to recall the grandeur and the conflicts of her past and for me to listen:

'And, I know people find this very hard to believe – of course, so few people have *any idea* what these competitions are like – I've seen young men *faint* on the *platform*, they were that keyed up.'

'Of course, in my bee-yoo-tiful home at (that place like Cake Icing again) I only had to play for my own pleasure in the *draw*-ring room. . . .'

'Over three hundred competitors, if you can believe that, and you couldn't afford to play a note out of place. I've seen grown men *sobbing* like babbies, if you can believe that, and I know *so* few people have any *idea* what these competitions. . . .'

I heard every little anecdote week after week, and said Hmmm and Phew, and preferred this situation to pounding through scales. What was more strange, and eerily so, was that as often as not *he* and their two children would also be sitting in the room, all silent even in breathing, hearing this white-lipped voice repeating her refrains for the ten-thousandth time. None of them ever interrupted these recollections, or laughed at, applauded or sneered at them, or expressed the slightest knowledge of them. The voice pick-pecked on; the broad, dark, unsmiling old workhorse of a husband sat staring at nothing; and the children, the bulbous Vera with the hundredweight of blonde hair and the over-dainty little Don with the ice-cream-cone knees, read their comics without a rustle or a hiccup. Sometimes there would be the noiseless exchange of Film Fun for Dandy or of Butterscotch for sugar-mint. It was like being preached at in church by a tomtit.

The recurring drama in Mrs Pearson's life was provided by the delicate balance of Vera's health. Vera looked to me as if she could knock a shed over with one blast of breath hurled from those beach-ball breasts. But Vera was very pale as well as ample in the flesh, and the dizzy spells which came over her without warning and without reference to time and place could disrupt the blandest circumstances. The chronic imminence of her daughter's collapse was a burden that Mrs Pearson carried with relish. When she talked about it her eyes and mouth opened and shut on the words with the fluttering of a bad actress doing Joan of Arc at the stake.

'With a *heart*, you see, you just never know,' she would say. 'People just can't *believe*. But the times it's happened. Just *flop*, like that. "Mother, I feel funny again," she says to me, and then *flop* without another word. People just don't know what to do, if I'm not there. They want to lay her down, and that's the *worst* thing for her kind of heart. You have to *sit* them down, you know. The times we would have lost her if I hadn't been there.' Mrs Pearson would do her goldfish mouth, and her eyes would be sucked in and blown out again, and she would settle her sigh upon the room as if popping a tea-cosy over it.

This repeated snatching from the hand of sudden death made a glamorous figure of Vera. I thought of her sometimes as some unfortunate princess cursed by the wicked fairy who wasn't invited to the christening. Mrs Pearson, it was true, made an unlikely *good* fairy, with that tart manner and the orderly hairdresser's curls like a row of nuts and bolts round her head; but she was the only one available for the role.

As with Mrs Pearson's descriptions of her own trials and torments Vera and the rest of the family listened to these accounts of emergency and resuscitation without the slightest show of interest. The family seemed to be held fast as an audience of figurines by Mrs Pearson's performance. There appeared never to be any raised voices in the house; but this thin, humourless personality, wrapped in its self-mesmerization, sustained a kind of government-by-filli-buster: click-clack, pick-peck, the house was drugged into submission by the unrelenting monologue. Our musical education advanced infinitesimally. My sister concentrated her efforts into perfecting an off-by-heart playing of an inordinately vulgar Victorian floriform called The Maiden's Prayer; I hunted down Chopin's shortest prelude and attacked it at the rate of a chord a week.

But the tragic Vera was, so to speak, given the full sonata treatment as the months went by. The more she ripened in breast, buttock and shoulder the darker were her mother's fears for her life, the more tremulous the accounts of the most recent funny feeling:

'Well, I think it was the worst she'd ever had. White as a sheet, she was. She didn't say a word, but I could tell. People stopped. I'm sure they didn't believe me. "She's not to be laid down, it's *fatal*," I told them. It's heart and chest combined you know now. Anything could happen at any time at all. As it was we were just outside Rose's café, so I got a man to help us inside. Vera had a rest and a milkshake. One of these days it will be the last, you know. White as a *sheet. . . .*'

The fire dribbled black slugs down its lower lip, the figurine family stared dumbly in the half-light, my fingers played Chopin chords on my knees.

A passing pair of pitboots belched through the net curtains, and my music teacher said how different life had been in that place that sounded like Cake Icing where she had been ever so private in her bee-yoo-tiful home.

The supreme sins in my chapel-goers' world were drinking and betting. Drinking was the more 'low', because of the carelessness it encouraged in matters of public conduct such as speech, dress and control of the bodily gasses; but betting was the deeper wickedness, because it broke up homes, sending the furniture to the pawnbroker and the wife to the canal, and made the children's bones rot for lack of regular meals.

These twin evils were embodied definitively in the brazen figure of Two Ton Titley who lorded the streets on Satan's behalf with a massive jocosity. I seldom saw him when he was not dressed, winter and summer, in a navy-blue double-breasted suit, the trousers hitched up high over the paunch so that it swelled smooth against the cloth, a pair of shiny black boots and a new-looking brown hat with a curly brim. Usually both hands would be deep in his trouser pockets and the jacket flapping back behind his wrists so that the imposing body, with its belt and braces stretched by every breath, was thrust at the disapproving and the envious alike with a royal disregard for sensibilities.

Mr Titley was a very big man; the buckle of his belt was on a level with some women's chins and his red neck, which was clamped into a collar only in the evenings, always attracted me by its particular show of strength – a bucket-shaped neck that folded its heavy skin when it moved. He was also a noisy man; he laughed frequently, with a rasp that suppressed conversation as he passed, and he talked always in a hoarse shout like a railway guard with a cold. He was nearly always walking from the pub to the club, or the other way round, and he farted often. These emissions were among the local wonders. To be the wrong side of Two Ton Titley at the moment of blasting was to be enveloped in a smell you could punch holes through in the air. He was disgusting, and apparently very happy.

Mr Titley was not just a drinking man who bet on horses. His sinfulness was the unforgivable kind: he *took* bets, and thus was one of the key men in the wickedness. There was a recurrent tut-tutting about him, a shaking of Sunday-best, hensrump hats at the mention of his name – in the same list as Lord Haw-Haw, Mussolini and Mrs Oojah's tarty daughter – when the jurors held their courts of morals over tea and slabcake. He was not a full-scale bookmaker, with an office or a big money bag and a portable stand with his name painted on it; he worked outside the law, as it then was applied, collecting his bets at the bar, employing one or two off-work runners to scurry from one street corner to another picking up more, and adding up his sums in his own kitchen.

Once I understood the nature of this illegal operation I was fascinated to watch it: Two Ton swaggering, full of confidence and purpose, around his territory, grating out a joke here and a jaunty, obscene insult there as he passed his customers smoking over the sports page on their front steps; one of his ferrets, never with much mental faculty and usually with a white muffler knotted at the throat, scuttling into a little group huddled in an entry and screwing up bits of paper and ten shilling notes and stuffing them in his pockets, then hurrying off to three heads poked through some front-room window for more slips and a handful of halfcrowns, then away again sucking through his teeth, short-cutting through backyards and broken fences and over the corners of gardens and down alleys to pause and peer from behind a shed a couple of backdoors down from Two Ton's house to make sure the police weren't making one of their periodic raids. It was an exhilarating, mouth-drying game to follow this messenger.

Two Ton attracted hangers-on, and he was seldom in the street on his own. He was the gurgling, guffawing centre of an uncertain circle that drew arrogance from his presence. People made way on the pavement when this snorting group came ambling and jostling along. They never appeared to be involved in fights, yet they were intimidating, suggestive of violence.

There was a power, an allurement in Two Ton's gross insolence. He was admired and censured for being the working man who was escaping work. There were clearly hard times for him, presumably when there was no racing, because he sometimes appeared in pit clothes, as big and as formidable as ever but quieter, half-spirited. He might have invented the old joke, frequently trotted out at the time, about work being the curse of the drinking classes.

He was, of course, the promoter of the pitch-and-toss school, which was portable so as to keep it from embarrassing the law. I saw it in operation on the recreation field: a ring of men, flushed and intent, throwing the coins and shouting numbers and alternating between yells of delight and grumpy muttering. It was incomprehensible, except that it clearly had to do, literally, with the wanton recklessness I had heard talked about with such distaste: it was throwing good money after bad. Two Ton did not appear to be throwing anything. He was holding money in large quantity. He was the pivot around which the other men conducted themselves. They brought him coins and notes, and sometimes he gave them some back. He kept up an encouraging, belching banter, his puce face prickly with pinheads of sweat nestling in its creases. 'C'mon, lads, yer luck's in. Doa be frit. The wife woa know.' He had money in his hands, in his pockets and often between his teeth and tucked between his trousers-top and his swelling midriff. 'That's the way, lads. Naow we can see ooz married to the moonishun wairkers. . . .'

He was a picture of godlessness, rampant with beer and blatant in his love of money – of the feel of it, of its corrupting desirability. He was immodesty personified. He was wicked. I hung about the ring of men with other boys, poking our heads between serge thighs, being told to piss off with impatience but no insistence, breathing in the improper drinking men's smell of the Gents and cigarette ends. Two Ton looked gigantic and unassailable in this setting. He was at work, selling sin with a grand flair:

'Yo'm a lucky bugger, Dick. Black Market stockings for that wench o' yourn, eh? Keep it goin', lads. Yo'm all gunna be quids in tudaye.'

I had a new word in my head, seized on from a chapel-goers' conversation and carried away into the secret places of my sermons to vast congregations, those pulpits inside my skull from which I held thousands spellbound. Blackguard. Two Ton was the ultimate blackguard.

I was at the bus-stop near my home one day, in the usual queue of spitters and grumblers, when one of the women pointed in the direction of the familiar gaggle as it came round the bend in the road, its laughter more visible than audible as the big figure in the front put his chin in the air with some joke. 'Bless 'im,' said the woman. 'Yo could never mistake my old man. Yo can tell 'im a mile off with that big belly. Ah, bless 'im.'

It was the gentleness that astounded me more than the passion. To find that Two Ton was loved and could be tenderly regarded was barely believable.

The gang reached us before the bus. Two Ton ambled past, as we made an avenue for him and the entourage, and he nodded his jowls at his wife without a word. 'Bless 'im.' she said, and wriggled her bust with pride.

There was a darker kind of drinking than the Two Ton gang's that I knew about. Poor, broken Mr Geary was our tragic genius – a casualty of the war of living, his pride surrendered in bitterness, his self-disgust progressively over-growing his personality, physical decay advanced beyond control. This was the demonic face of the bottle. Mr Geary was not guilty, but possessed.

I used to see him tottering gauntly in the street, coming away from the pub, a shabby man but not an untidy one. He always had a tie on and his buttons and laces done up. He was stooped and pale, and both the posture and the colour exaggerated the broad bulge of his forehead and the straggle of the receded, sandy hair about his ears. It was an intelligent face, and sad. As he made his hesitant way home, one hand extended always to one side as if reaching for a handrail, he would veer into people, apologizing sometimes in an almost tearful mumble and at others with an elaborately precise enunciation, using their names as if to prove his faculty of recognition:

'Sorry, Missis *Bur-ton* . . . My fault, *Ed-gar*. . . . Sorry, *Beryl*, Cock . . .' He would try to smile if he bumped into a child.

Sober, he was noticeably trembly but also self-assured in a distant, curt way, and people treated him carefully, and in some cases even with deference. It struck me as very like the way invalids were treated when they first appeared in the street after some long illness, except that Mr Geary was not patronized as much.

How much of what I came to 'know' about him had any reality? It must have contained the distortions of people's sentimentality, excuse, pity and contempt; but it had the appeal of a romantic truth.

The district had known desperate, persecuting poverty, which its people had not been able to overthrow. (The war put an end to it; but years of a prevailing sense of helplessness left their mark in attitudes. Boys I played with used to sing, unthinking, an ironic little song that had been handed down to them and which began: 'Oh, Aby, mi lad, You ought to be *glad*, Yer fairther's got a job . . .') The people needed to explain their own defeat. Mostly they could blame the harsh greed of the coal owners. But that was not quite enough. Humiliation had brought guilt, and guilt needed expiation. They could blame some of their own kind, some of the union officials, for incompetence and timidity. They transferred their *self*-pity, their acknowledgement of failure, to the sacrificial figure of Mr Geary, who had been the cleverest, the most militant, the most bitter of all the rank and file. Mr Geary was now committing a drawn-out, public self-abasement on their behalf.

He had been the coalface lawyer, the self-taught man of letters, the bookworm with a hundred authors' names and a thousand lines of poetry on his tongue, the brilliant talker and boss-baiter with a vicious cutting edge to his jokes. He had been the home-grown marvel who was going to mount a rostrum of orange boxes at every street corner and rouse the people to action. He was tall and bright-eyed and had straight, firm good looks, good biceps and a well rewarded confidence with girls. He was liked as well as respected.

When the pits laid men off he was the men's spokesman, more trusted than the union officials, more fiery, more resourceful. But he would not take nomination for a union post, insisting that he was never going to be 'a tame gaffer's man' and that he was more valuable preparing himself for a future career in national politics. He was laid off himself —victimized as a trouble maker by the coal owners and resented as an embarrassment by the union. He was in and out of work, spent more and more time talking for free beer in the pubs, reading through the wet mornings in his kitchen, wandering broodily about the fields in the afternoons. The years drifted by in a demoralizing sequence of work and idleness, outbursts of verbal passion in the pub and at the miners' meetings, mental depression, sulky submissiveness leading to more work, then idleness again. Life went sour in every aspect. A child was born crippled in the legs; he began the repetitive coughing of the irreversible miners' chest disease. Now he was in his middle forties and looked sixty, drank on pocket money from his wife, who was working, and on handouts from friends, prospering from the war, who remembered his promise and his status among them. It did not take a great deal of drink to numb him now. He was not an alcoholic in the sense of sustaining himself compulsively on drink; he used it as a tranquillizing drug, to weight him down, to burden himself permanently in a scoffing, sardonic penance.

His old strength still lingered about him when he was with his friends. He might have been a blind ex-boxing champion or maimed footballer. He could still talk sharply, cleverly and with enough bite, in the hour before the drink submerged his brain, to deter much attempt at teasing, although younger men were beginning to laugh at him openly.

He read newspapers closely, the quick mind assimilating what took others in the pub in the mornings twice as long to grasp, and he would interpret the between-the-lines meaning with his daily lecturettes on the progress of the war and the unlikelihood of any lasting good coming out of it in the end for the working man. He was still a firebrand at heart, the men said of him, and argued loudly about whose turn it was to buy him the next beer.

There came a day when a major change had to be made in this affecting picture of a flawed man of talent wrecked by pernicious fate. I heard that he frequently beat his crippled daughter after his drinking bouts. The sheer unfairness of this appalled me. He no longer appeared pitiable but brutal. The twisted half-smile as he came stumbling diagonally across the pavement, and the tremulous scowling of his sober mornings, took on less innocent significance. I began to imagine the scene at home which separated these two appearances, and it was a grim enough episode I invented: the white-faced, lurching drunk punching wildly at the sobbing girl with the iron clamps on her legs. I took to crossing the road to get out of his way when I saw him.

Then I heard an extraordinary comment about Mr Geary, which adjusted his position again to place him in the ambiguous role between victim and villain. It came out of a conversation among some patient, ruminating women in a queue for potatoes. 'Ee blames 'imself for that giarl, yo know,' one of them said. '*And* eez got a right to, if yo ask me. That's why ee takes it out on 'er when eez drunk. . . . They say ee cries like a babby the next morning.'

❧ 5 ❧

Crimes and Games

An inflamed, collective resentment took hold of a gang of
us on a morning of great heat. We were right at the Equator
of our summer holiday, becalmed in boredom, the sweat
like hot toffee on our eyelids. We sat in the gathered
powder-dust of the gutter, cooling our ankles in it, and
sucked hard and deep on the smell of the sizzling tar in the
way the men drew on their Woodbines when they were
considering the bleak in their lives. We wanted revenge for a
lifetime of hurts never less defined and never more intolerable than they were now, congealed and smouldering
purple in our heads. We were never more safe from each
other; never more united in rebellion.

The day was nervous of us. An old woman put her
shrunken, parrot's head out of an upstairs window, stared
and shivered and withdrew, shutting herself in behind the
sash and the curtains and then peeping until we gave her the
killer-glower. We turned our eyes on a dog lying swollen at
the foot of a garden wall, and he blinked in fear, rose and left.
No birds sang.

We felt our dark strength. We were building a group
tension in silence. Deliberately one boy poked a forefinger
into a tiny hole in his sock and pulled to make an irreparable
split; another tore off the loose sole of one of his shoes,
grinning. We were establishing a mood, a key. It would
dominate everything, giving purpose and significance to

what was to come next. We were sunk in a black conspiracy: primitives offering our souls on the altar of this evil, mad-making sun. When he was totally in possession of us, so that our heads would be close to bursting with the tension, his directive would come suddenly from the mouth of one of us, who would then have the mystical status of leader for the day to be inspired with invention in the dark arts.

The spirit moved, and voice came loud and sharp. It was big John's. 'The Bluebell Wood', he said, and we got up immediately and trotted in a tight bunch behind him, grim for pleasure where we were not allowed to go. Smeared with sweat and dust, Arab-brown from the sun, our thin clothes rolled up heroically tight under armpits and groin, we were like some scrawny band of dwarf mendicants seized abruptly by desire for pillage, and intent on the gardens of the rich.

On we went, clip-slap in the tropical burn, ignoring any shade, our unity a deeply sensual pleasure as we held our places one-for-all in the devotion to big John's pace. We left the houses, reached the brilliant yellow lane smelling ripe-rotten and soft of its bulging hedges like the old velvet of sitting-room cushions, went under the railway bridge with its chapel-porch damp, and then we were at the first of our targets. DANGER, the sign said in metal letters on a pole, and TRESPASSERS WILL BE PROSECUTED, and it added other information about unauthorized persons and fines. It would be a day of such signs.

We were in the denied playground, Authority's land of culverts, pipes, ditches, iron-handled manholes, concealed clefts and gaps in the earth, swamp and smoking slag, rusted blades and springs that could leap suddenly underfoot and slash a leg. This was the dumping ground for the rubbish of the pit. It was a minefield stuffed with buried treasure: strange-shaped locks and keys, huge chain links, ratchet ends, vast and charred timbers, lumps of stuff

neither metal nor vegetable and pulpy like some mysterious
animal corpse, coins, boots, lamps. And all this was overgrown with tall grass and tough weeds, which now had spiky
flowers on them as brash and unpretty as ourselves. And
there was a point where the grass and the weeds merged into
a wood with a wire fence round it, a stream to be found deep
inside it, and the spongy beds of bluebells. The KEEP OUT
signs were here as well.

We treated the place perhaps more like a fairground than
a playground; we had a go on everything. We started with
the big black water pipe, a long slug with a drooping-down
end, which came out of the tall slagheap and ran for an
inviting cricket-pitch length to make a T-junction with a
shorter one open at both ends. To crawl the length of the
short one and plop out at the other end was a light scamper;
to turn off at the junction and penetrate deep into the blackness of the long one, which ended God knew where, was a
piece of brave devilry that could command respect. We went
in, heads up against rumps, being kicked in the chest but
preferring the comfort of the physical contact to the terror
of being left behind in that cold, tight tunnel stinking of
slime and the secrets of the underworld.

How far did we get? Half a mile? Five yards? Those of us
who quaked well back in the queue, where daylight was still
glimmering behind, could moan in a pretence of impatience,
but we were glad big John said there was something in the
way and we'd have to squiggle backwards and out again.
We danced on top of the pipe, plump Geof with the yellow
curls doing his obscene hula-hula girl rotations which would
have earned him a whack from his father at home, and we
climbed on each other's backs to swing on the DANGER
sign.

Big John led his pack through the grass and the bushes of
weeds, kicking at the half-buried metal, and we tore loose

bits free and swiped off the heads of thistles with them. We found some broken glass and smashed it further into splinters. We found a boot without a toe-end, and took turns in wearing it, one-legged giants trampling down the nettles, then agreed to take it into the wood with us to see if it would sail like a canal barge in the stream. All the time the sun blazed its intoxication on us. We were its creatures, and we saw no-one else.

We went through the wire fence and chopped at the KEEP OUT sign with our iron tubes and lumps of wood and the boot. We pushed our way through the brambles and branches, rolled in the damp sponge under the bluebells, and fell into the stream face down with our knees in the mud. The water tasted stale and sickening, worse than licking a desk lid; but it was pleasant to stamp through, and to kick in each other's faces. Then we decided to dam it, and hung three-at-a-time on thick branches to tear them off with a creak and a sudden snap that dropped us in a heap; and we hunted the undergrowth for stones and old wood, soaking wet and as soft as lettuce underneath.

Tiredness hit us unforeseen and all at once, when the dam was half finished and someone vomited through sucking too much of the long grass with the sweet gold stem.

So we sat on the bank, among the smooth, warm tree roots where they stuck out like the curled legs of front-room tables, and savoured the richness of our criminality. We had trespassed, stolen, invaded and destroyed. A calm settled on us. The sun had pulled away to one side, and had withdrawn much of its fire.

So, still disciplined and inter-dependent, we grouped and went home, with mud dry on us and leaves down our shirts. And as we got near to the houses we were met by a woman in a state of fury. Her face was crimson and her eyes wild. She was Don and Geof's mother, and now for the first time our ranks were broken. Geof ran spontaneously to meet her, the curls matted with twigs and the smile crystal in a face not unlike a small, dried, cow's pancake. 'We've 'ad the *Police* out looking for you lot,' she screamed, and she put both hands on her hip bones and glared at us.

The announcement sent a surge of thrill and satisfaction through us. We looked from one to another with flushes of pride. We could break up now, and we did, running for home.

'Do you know it's nearly four o'clock?' my mother said to me, amused, when I arrived. 'Your dinner's dried up to a frazzle.'

I went round to see Don and Geof later, and found Geof swinging on the front garden gate. He said he had to stay on the inside of it. Don, he said, had been belted with the frying pan, because he was the older one, and was not being let out of the house.

Don's face then appeared at one of the windows. We nodded at each other with a formal, adult familiarity, like a pair of club members with some long distant memory of close ties.

Crime was in our minds a good deal, intermittently but reliably, like other background certainties such as variety shows on the radio and our rations of sweets. It had a furtive appeal to me, as an improper entertainment, which must have had much to do with the way in which I learned most about it — from the newspapers.

I was by now reading indiscriminately, taking in whatever happened to come in front of my gaze, and I could no more resist reading the words on the backs of dinner plates and on a cereal packet called Force — every cereal, other than porridge, was referred to as The Force in our house for years, even after this particular one had disappeared from our breakfasts – than I could resist my Champion comic or sugar sandwiches. It was mostly, of course, the satisfying *expertise* of reading that made me so avid. But in some of the material which was not aimed deliberately at my age group I found this special, tangy excitement.

I would read the *News Chronicle* and the local weekly paper from the top left-hand corner of the front page to the bottom right-hand one of the back, much of the contents simply going through my system like a dose of verbal liver salts, scarcely touching my sides: the words were all and often nothing. But accounts of war battles, if they had detail of places, death rolls and weapons, held my attention, and reports of crime did so even more firmly. They did not disturb.

In those days of small newspapers with terse reports, crime came to us mostly in tightly condensed accounts of court cases. So crime to me, while it could be violent and callous, was nearly always punished; the fact added to the spice of crime's appeal. So much that was desirable was forbidden. I sensed that much was being left unsaid; the archness of the reports did their job, which was to intrigue the reader, to tickle his lusts while assuming a peremptory, detached tone. Crime was wrong, but it was common to so many people it seemed something that ought to be experienced.

We destroyed the pavilion in an exuberant wilfulness, far more playful and yet far more brutal than our rape of the Bluebell Wood, which had had a ceremonial solemnity. Razing the pavilion on one of the early nights of late autumn, when the cold, blue-grey air made us alert and precise, was a clear-cut, objective crime, committed for the pleasure it would bring.

'We' in this instance were a different group: three times

as many, and with a majority of older boys, some of them already at work. There had been an interference with our sovereignty on the recreation field. There had been some organized football played by adult strangers in full gear, and we had found ourselves pushed aside for some days, even locked out at one entrance, although that had merely caused the irritation of a long walk round to the other for those who did not have gardens backing onto this blessed plot of ours. There was a tart, tense, irked feeling in the air. We were not brooding or surly, but impatient, combative. The aggression would turn inwards on victims inside the group if some other target was not found for it soon.

Eyes and limbs tingled in the restive dusk.

When the mob turned on the pavilion the action was not spontaneous. There was the manufactured clarity of tactics about it. We went first at the windows with stones and sticks, working in teams, and then threw the objects we needed for heavier damage out from inside. There were a couple of long, narrow benches, to be used as battering rams, a fire fender, a poker, sturdy old chairs to be broken up for use as clubs. We might have wreaked havoc more quickly by pursuing the assault from the inside. But that did not have as much appeal as crushing the victim methodically from outside. It seemed important to batter the place *in*. That was more blatant, more controlled, more criminal.

The pavilion had long ago fallen into decrepitude. It was rarely used, thick with dust, its sparse furniture split and shaky; the only equipment in it was beyond repair, like an old clock on a wall, a tattered, basketwork skip, a cricket pad in shreds. But it was intact, if precariously, as a building, with its doors on hinges and a set of pigeon-hole lockers on a wall. The mob beat it to the ground.

There developed quickly a laughing but curiously cold exhilaration. It needed concentration and persistence to man the battering rams and wear down the doors and the wooden walls:

'Okaye, Sammy, Fred, Les, our Tommy in the front. Yo want to keep in step if yo can, so yo can run straighter.'

'Okaye, 'ave a breather naow. Your turn next, Spuggie, in the front. All run together.'

A door went in with a great slap. We broke through a wall to a cheer. We were trampling broken glass and splintered wood, and coughing in the heavy dust. We were never in a rage.

The point came when the roof was sagging in conflicting angles over the raggedly gaping walls, and through the dust and the urgency of the activity we could see the wounds we had made in a place which had been as familiar and as much spoken about as a person in our lives. I began to feel uneasy. Obviously before long the pavilion would collapse to rubble. I did not feel I could follow this destruction through.

I found myself with others of the younger ones, hanging back in an apprehensive huddle. It was fully night now, but light enough for the shapes of the ruin and the wreckers to be standing out, grey on grey in a busy blur. The older ones had left us behind; had advanced the game into concerted vindictiveness. The corrugated iron was clanking and teetering, jagged and buckled. There was danger in the crime now. The faces round me were white and scared, and I could feel my own skin stretching thinly on my bones in the cold. We left in the same huddle on sudden impulse. The bangs and thumps and low voices were muffled by night at our backs, and we shrank into our small individual selves as we sidled home separately, composing a look of ease and normality to cover a major guilt.

The incident created a brief but impressive stir in the district. Policemen came to my school, talking earnestly to teachers, asking stern questions of whole classes of us. We gave them chanted answers in an infant singsong such as we had not used for years: 'Noaw, Sir. . . . At 'ome, Sir.'

Some boys were questioned separately, a couple of them among those of us who had been present, and their flushed monosyllables were indistinguishable from those of the genuinely innocent, who undoubtedly knew some of the culprits but lied automatically. We were an unbreachable mutual protection society in the face of authority, at least as long as authority had no direct accusations to make at individuals. That called for more nerve than some of us possessed. But it never applied in this case. Numerous visits were made by the policemen to the homes of some of the working youths involved, and there was dark muttering about arrests and people being sent away to reform schools. Nothing of the kind happened.

The ruin, which had a short period of celebrity, was soon being shrugged out of mind. The thing would have fallen down before long of its own accord, people said; they had more important things to worry about, they added, implicating the police in the pursuit of triviality. There was a war on, wasn't there?

The fear of the crime receded from me. The night was resolved in my memory as a taste of important conspiracy. The guilt that lingered was of regret at running away.

My family were victims of a crime. We suffered trespass and theft in circumstances which were pleasingly dramatic, at any rate on later consideration.

It would be late September or early October, and around midnight or after. I woke up alone in the bed I shared with my brother to a house full of breathless indignation. More than that, there was a sense of impending violence which was unique in it.

'Arthur, Arthur!' My mother was shouting my father's

name, not my own, as I could recognize by the tone. Then, as I burst out of the bedclothes, dragging them behind me in the confused dark, I heard her again:

'I think they've gone. Arthur, Arthur!'

Doors rattled and banged. It was the back door, that second one.

I was suddenly aware, although by intuition because I was now on the landing and could not see what was happening, that my father was rushing into the back garden.

The critical word had not been spoken since I had woken up, but I said it aloud with instant conviction now that I understood the indignation downstairs: APPLES!

I ran back into the bedroom, which was at the back of the house, and pulled open the curtains. There was light from the living-room window spilling over the outside steps and the rockery and the lawn. But I could not see any movement. I opened the window and pushed my head out, the blood beating hard in my temples. I could hear rustlings of foliage and feet hitting hard surfaces – the fence, probably. I blundered across the room to the drawer where I kept important matter, such as money and conkers, and snatched out the little flashlight that was in it. Its beam shone into the window of night to reveal nothing but itself. Frustration was dominating the episode. There was another bang of a door.

'Well?'

'Two, I think. They've gone. I nearly caught one. They were going over the fence.'

The house chattered with outrage and wonder. I started downstairs to join in, considered the likelihood of being allowed to stay, and sat down halfway instead. I listened captivated to a switchbacking, jigsaw-like conversation out of which I reconstructed the story of the raid on our apple trees.

We had five or six of them, one bent-up old one which

could be climbed and swung from, and which produced a rich crop of Orange Pippins, and the others younger, much smaller, whose fruit was greener. From the six of them we could expect to gather every year a harvest that filled every spare corner in the house. Gathering, packing and storing was a ritual that took a lot of time. We ended with boxes and trays and tins of apples, each wrapped in newspaper and each layer separated by more newspaper, and we were assured of apple pie, apple pudding, apple sauce, apple crumble, and plain raw apple until deep into the winter.

Now, apple snatching from other people's gardens was a local skill of traditional lore. Scrumping was a sport of the season more than a minor crime, and as such it had rules and conventions. It was essentially a boy's prerogative, to begin with, which meant that a youth could not expect to remain acceptable at scrumping beyond the point of, say, his first half-year at work. In terms of haul, the line was drawn at what a scrumper could carry away on his person – that is, in his pockets and down his shirt, which could mean a considerable amount if an older brother's too-big shirt was borrowed for the occasion, and perhaps in his cap; the terms of reference did not permit carrier bags, sacks or any other receptacle.

In return for the observance of these rules the owners of apple trees tacitly undertook not to invoke the police or any outside party, such as a headmaster, if they spotted and recognized a scrumper or caught one. But penalty was admitted. The owner could fairly clout an ear or a backside, summarily at the moment of seizure, and could march the captive down to his own home for presentation in a misery of shame to his father, when the punishment was fully understood by everyone to be for getting caught. Apple-tree owners were not permitted to deliver any full-scale beatings of their own.

What had happened in the case of our trees was not covered by the standing agreement on scrumping. The hour of day ruled it out immediately. Then there was the character of the thieves. They could only be guessed at, but one of them was plainly an adult, because of his size and shape and the sound of his voice, and the younger one was uncertainly placed in his middle teens. It looked like a partnership of father and son or of two brothers, and there were numerous families which could have supplied it. Conclusively, they had carried sacks. It would have been a case for the police, had we any certainty of identity.

They had timed the raid well, as they thought. The apples would be close to harvest; a week later we might have stripped the trees. But they badly miscalculated in another way. This non-drinking, religious, quietly spoken household stayed up late, as was jokingly said among relatives, to the point of vice. If the thieves found a darkened, still house and assumed the family snoring into the second hour or so of sleep they were misinformed. Around midnight to one o'clock my parents would barely have finished reading, sewing, doing chapel paper work, before committing themselves to prayer and sleep. So when the partners came slithering over the fence from the recreation field, and stealing through the hedge, and began fumbling and scraping their feet and muttering around the trees, my parents' ears and noses went up in countryman's throwback sensitivity to foreign presence among the crops, and the game was up.

My father had hurtled down the stairs and out into the garden with what must have been to these local thieves a most surprisingly aggressive impetus. His gentle manner was notable in a harsh environment; and he was not a big man. But honest anger, a sense of home and family threatened, had transformed his style. The thieves fled, with enough yelps and grunts of alarm to give us the information we had about their approximate ages. The chase was brief and frantic over a treacherous obstacle course on a dark night with mist in it.

Hearing this drama recounted in a haphazard, piecemeal way, so that I could fasten on to little bits of detail and fit them into place, I was thrilled by a picture of my father in a setting of personal violence that had never occurred to me before. I put my eyes on my knees, hunched on the stairs, and pondered the revelation. . . .

'You're supposed to be in bed, aren't you?' The voice was as composed and as elegant as when he prayed in the pulpit.

The murder of Little Roy was not planned over a long period, although when it was done it seemed as if it had been in my mind all my life. There was a feeling of something long nagging now settled: a labour accomplished.

Little Roy was a particularly neat, groomed, noiseless boy, compressed and smooth, as if shaped on a lathe. Head, wrists, hands and legs had a perfect miniature consistency, and his clothes were an exact fit. He appeared among us from time to time, or usually a bit to one side, sliding quickly into the games, giving no offence, making no mistakes, readily accepted and not missed when he withdrew in his own time. I had no feelings about him. He was Little Roy.

I was in the field on my own, marooned in vagueness on one of those sepia, indeterminate days without a season, and I saw him come in from the other side. I made the decision to murder him immediately.

I stood up on the bank and waved, and then began running over to meet him. He kept on towards me, without changing that crisp little pace of his.

We met, and said hello. He was unblemished as always, the skin clean, his short hair almost white, a green jacket close on his shoulders.

'Follow my leader,' I said, and set off towards the big, hummocky grass that could be bounced on with both feet. Then I led on towards the far corner, to jump some nettles, crawl through some brambles, jump from side to side of the ditch. He stayed deferentially behind, nimble and serene.

I ran halfway up the bank from the ditch, stopped and turned and ran back at him. When I held him as hard as I could round the chest he was still compact and self-assured. 'What you doing?'

'Gunna murder you.'

I was much the bigger, and I put him on the ground quickly. We rolled and wrestled, and I caught glimpses of his face. At last the ease and control were gone. There were surprise, discoloration, objection there.

But the small, glossy body was firm and quick. He was resourceful, evasive, not attempting to punch or kick but concentrating on getting away, with wriggles and twists. He closed up into a ball of head, knees and arms, so that he was slippery and gripless, then uncoiled suddenly to dart away. I grabbed a leg and dropped on top of him again, smelling our sweat and the strong damp of the grass. Neither of us spoke.

He was weakening, and I found the way. By using my weight, lying flat on his chest and face, pulling at the grass to give myself leverage, I was making him gasp and tremble. I held the position until I was half-dizzy, then pushed myself up and back and put both hands round his throat. He stared up with white lips and red eyes. I finished him.

It was like strangling a bird. The flesh yielded softly to my fingers. I squeezed tears out of his eyes: small tears in the inside corners.

When I stood up he was still astonishingly tidy, while I was aware of my own dishevelment. But he was certainly dead. I left him lying in the grass. It was yellow and torn where we had been fighting, surrounded by a dull green.

I saw him often afterwards. He came to the fringe of the group, the face and character as cool and secret as ever before, and he raised no complaint. I had murdered him, and that was the end of it. I had been murdered by others, and I had taken my turn.

Late autumn was the time of the games. A 'game' was a special classification, separate from the improvisations known as 'playing' and from football and cricket, which carried the grave requirements of written law. Our games had formality, although we came to them naturally without having to learn rules. We grew into them, like spoken language. They belonged to late autumn by the logic of custom and because they could be used to exploit the season. They could have been played equally well at some other times of the year, but hardly ever were. Autumn had the tone for them.

It was dark long before bedtime; but the smell of mist was appetising, unsettling; there were intimations of winter in the chill flick and shove of the wind; there was urgency in our need to use this free time out of doors while it was still manageable, before the wet black of winter forced us inside. It challenged us. We responded.

The blackout was no longer a matter to be observed scrupulously in our district. But if chinks of light were tolerated flashing beams could still excite policemen and air-raid precaution wardens and lots of other adults with leanings toward public responsibility. So there was added a deeply satisfying, extra danger to the nightly episodes of Dicky, Dicky Shine the Light.

The game was close to the proportions of a tournament. It was no slight, single-night affair; it could take a week to work through it, the tension building all the time. The framework was utterly simple: one boy with an electric torch, the rest scattered and calling him to catch and identify them in the glare of the light. But among these terraces, with alleys, yards, dustbin alcoves, outhouses, dog kennels, rain-tubs, hedges, broken walls and dumped gas-stoves, all menacing with shadow in the sourly misted night, the hunt was elaborate with stealth and deception. The torch had to be used sparingly, to conserve the battery and to delay interference from adults. We had great skill in hiding, using the shapes of shadow, calling the name and running full-speed into some blind blackness, inviting a chase. Timidity meant failure. Chance could be calamitous: a door suddenly opened to let out a wedge of light; an irritated dog; a loose tin can accidentally kicked.

Hiding is always accompanied by fear, even in games; the two instantly associate. In the dark even the most familiar setting can intimidate. Like all our games Dicky, Dicky was essentially an ordeal.

One night's session could have the torch changing hands three or four times, as someone was caught and became the hunter; or it could fail to produce a catch at all, perhaps broken up by a man in uniform or by parents. We would begin with a group of half a dozen or more and expect to have the torch in everyone's hands before we regarded the game as ended. It had an appeal to something in our inner nature: hunter and quarry; the animal use of camouflage; the sudden pounce.

Asked at home what I had been doing out there in the dark I would say, 'Playing hide and seek,' gloating over the fact that such a disarming name conveyed nothing of the intense, cunning competitiveness of our game. Hide and seek was for infants and jollity at home at Christmas. Dicky, Dicky was for our reputations, standing, self-esteem.

I had a flashlight in the shape of a pistol, a present from my older brother. It was a neat thing to hold, the lamp working when the trigger was pulled, and I rated it highly among my possessions. But for the purposes of Dicky, Dicky it proved a failure I hated to admit. Its simulation of a gun seemed excitingly appropriate to the game, but it was too toylike, the beam thin and short-ranged. I suppose this was an early lesson in how to disadvantage oneself in a contesting world by irrelevant aesthetic considerations. Much more effective was a bicycle headlamp, clumsy to carry and switch on and off but searching in its range, even with half the glass covered in insulating tape, which was common practice for wartime cyclists. I conceded the point grudgingly, after a long night of maddening futility with the pistol-light.

I had thought I would introduce some style into the game, firing like lightning from the hip. 'What yo doin' with them matches?' a woman yelled from her backdoor. I gave her a rapid burst. 'Yo daft bugger. Oo is it?' she yelled. 'George, there's someone in the yard with matches.'

Once a terrace was roused like that a session was over. We faded into the dark.

'Mardy!' someone hissed at me, as our shapes sped close and passed. 'Yo'm it agaairn tumorrer night.'

The pistol-light thumped in my pocket. It is not easy to sulk and sprint at the same time; but I managed it.

The imperative season. The breathless time. Our male society was at its most impatient. We needed to cram the hours with each other's company, before the winter imposed home on us and the shrill rule of mothers, sisters and sisters' friends. The women and girls had control indoors, because their skills and self-assurance were there. So we made fast for each other's protection while the calendar and the clock allowed.

Among us we had our club premises: a garden shed behind one house, a dug-out with a roof of household debris and sods of grass behind another, a den of old bath-tubs and chair-backs and potato sacks somewhere else. We hurried there through the tasty fog of dusk, and jammed in tight as a rush-hour bus. We took our Hotspurs, Wizards, Dandies, Film Funs, Champions, many of them crumbling at the touch through age and use, and swopped them with the acumen of Irish horse dealers for present enjoyment and future business. We made cigarettes out of discarded stubs and brown paper, and made up stories of minutely circumstantial indecency about local adults, and muttered and giggled them into each other's ears. Our faces changed colour and shape in the wavering candle light, so that we were suddenly silent in surprise and discovery.

But we preferred movement. At the centre of our exclusiveness was a restless need of competition. Physical resource was our most valued currency. In the dark and in the stadium of the back yard the contest had to be without the complications of equipment and disinterested adjudication. Requirements were met in the trial of strength and agility that went by the name of Humbug, Finger or Thumb? The only apparatus necessary was a firm wall, and we had walls in abundance.

Someone would lean over to make a 'horse' braced with feet apart and the palms of his hands flat against the brick. Sometimes there would be a team-mate to stand with his back to the wall, to act as a cushion for the horse's head, and sometimes not. Another boy would leap on the horse's back. He would hold his closed right fist in the air, with the thumb held down tightly under his forefinger, or hold up the forefinger or the thumb. The fist was the humbug. (Why the name? There was no explanation.) He would call out: 'Humbug, finger or thumb?' The boy bent against the wall would guess. If he was right the two changed places. If he was wrong another of us would leap up on top of him, to increase the weight and repeat the question. Given enough players we would have two teams, with two-man or three-man horses. A succession of incorrect guesses would result in a tottering heap of bodies clinging to each other until the legs of the horse buckled and the human pile collapsed. It was astonishing how much weight could be borne. If the boys piling on failed to hold their position, and slithered off, the boys making the back were considered to have won. To be the third or fourth – even fifth! – body on the horse was a tricky matter. It was not permitted for the jumpers to touch the wall to steady themselves. Again, the devotion to integrity was earnest. We didn't joke about our games.

It is easy to fall into the trap of romanticizing the more vivid activity in childhood, and magnifying its significance. But there seems to me to be something of special impress about those distant games. They reflect how truly we related to our environment. Their essence was our interdependence, our group self-sufficiency. We were not distracted from our proper preoccupations with each other and with tangible circumstances by the perpetual capsule entertainment of television and pop music, which has been directed at subsequent generations. There were no advertising jingles on our lips, and there were no puppet-figure products of an adolescence industry for us to impersonate. We were influenced by a non-exploiting reality, and made games out of it.

6

A Note on Home and Family

Both my parents were born during the last decade of the nineteenth century. They knew a vanished, pastoral England with the squire in the manor, the doctor in his pony trap, sides of bacon in the kitchen, an earth closet in the garden, paraffin lamps, and commonplace illiteracy and infant mortality.

My father was one of twelve children, the son of a farm manager, who later left farming to be a gardener. My father barely knew some of the older members of the family, because they had grown up and gone away to find work while he was still a small child. He lived in a house which was two small cottages converted into a big one, and there were four bedrooms. My mother was born in Cockney London, but went to live with her grandmother in my father's village – Fritwell, Oxfordshire – when she was still a baby, because of her mother's death. She stayed there until she was twelve, when she went back to London after her father remarried.

I never met any of my grandparents, but I gathered from an early age some indications of what they looked like and what kind of people they were. The clearest impression is of my mother's father, because he was the only grandparent I have seen in a photograph. He was a short, sturdy man, in heavy, dark clothes and with a thick, dark beard, and with kindly eyes. He could not read or write, except for his name –

Bates, which seemed to suit the unequivocal look of him –
but he owned houses and a fish and chip shop. He was
affectionate and generous to his three daughters, with sweets
and little presents, and he held firm opinions about the right
and wrong ways for people to conduct themselves. His home
was substantial and furnished in solid comfort, and its front
door had a large brass knob which my mother had to keep
brightly polished, because its shine was one of his particular
concerns. He was shrewd at business, sound at figures. The
image I have of his second wife is meagrely of a consciously
ladylike person, probably tall. I never heard my mother refer
to her in any terms other than 'Mrs Bates'.

Impressions of my paternal grandparents are even less
detailed: an always busy, always booted grandfather; an
even busier, permanently aproned, more talkative grandmother. These two figures are really no more than vague
representations. I don't remember hearing my father talk
much about them. As a child I needed to put shapes to them,
simply to complete a satisfactory picture of the Fritwell
household in my mind; but I did not find it necessary to
establish features, height or tone of character. I was much
more intrigued by the ambience of the village life. I was
fascinated by the references to horse-drawn charabancs;
carol-singing tours with lanterns on picturesque white
nights – the Christmas card come to life; the weekly Sunday
parade of bulky joints of roast beef which had to be cooked
for all those huge families by the village baker because they
were too big for the mothers' ovens. There was, it seems, an
irresistibly eccentric Aunt Jane, who made poleaxing alcohol
out of cowslip and other deceptive ingredients and who
tippled heartily, saying abrupt and unaccountable things to
people as they passed her cottage. There was a pompous
uncle who had done well for himself. There were rich men
with haughty voices who clattered through the village

on lofty horses, requiring people to move aside or be run down.

Horses were important everyday utilities. When my father went to work for the grocer at fourteen, orders were often collected and delivered by horse. When the first world war began he was put into the mounted machine-gun corps, and for much of the war he was on horseback in France. He must have been a good horseman, because he was a despatch rider for a long time. His was the generation plundered by that war, and he and my mother would sometimes list the young men they knew personally who were killed in it; it sounded like half a village. He was gassed, but not wounded. He used to tell us little stories about the fighting, the winters in the trenches, the lice; but he never dwelt long on the detail. I have noticed with other men of his age, with memories of gruesome privations during those four years, the same reticence in talking of them, the same lowering of the voice, the same muted bitterness that seems suppressed by re-summoned shock when the nightmare is recalled. A phrase of my mother's recurs in my mind when I remember these brief reminiscences of war from my father: 'We didn't know. We didn't know.'

My parents' married life was punctuated by so many moves from place to place, house to house, that as a child I found the sequence bewildering. There did not seem to me to have been enough years in the history of the world to accommodate them. There were Oxfordshire, Gloucestershire, Kent, Essex, London, Cannock; and during the twenty years I lived with my parents, having been born in Essex, I lived in six different houses, ranging from vault-like urban Victoriana to a country bungalow. They have since lived in three more, including a farm cottage with sagging oak beams and a tendency towards peremptory collapse of the walls. My brother and sister and I were born in different

towns. I have come to value the variety of this family background. It enabled me to assimilate early on, through overheard conversation, visits to and from distant friends and
exchange of letters, a haphazard but wide knowledge of the
look and feel of my own country. I travel well, uproot and
transplant equably.

The reasons for all those family moves were my father's
search for better-paid jobs and the insecurity of renting
houses from private landlords. My father worked in grocery
shops as an assistant or manager, until his retirement. The
wages seem to have been always poor, and the hours crim-
inally long, with all the clearing up that went on after closing
time. Both my parents appeared ceaselessly at work during
my childhood, manufacturing clouds of steam in the kitchen,
mending shoes, stitching clothes, digging gardens and
allotments, erecting rickety sheds, constructing occasional
tables out of boxwood and butter barrels, putting up shelves
and stirring cake-mix. There was a tightly budgeted self-
sufficiency in the house, with nothing wasted and next to
nothing saved. My mother was repeatedly saying: 'Ah, one
of these days . . .' and: 'Ah, when our ship comes in. . . .'

Laced into this industry and no doubt helping to sustain
confidence and peace of mind in it, was my parents' church
commitment. My father preached in some Methodist pulpit
either morning or evening on most Sundays, and we used to
make jokes about his habit of writing snippets of sermons on
bits of cheese paper or on the backs of old bills and envelopes,
wherever he happened to be about the house or shop at the
moment of inspiration, and then popping them into a flower
vase or under a tin of baked beans for later collection. He
took Sunday school every Sunday afternoon, and a boys' club
one evening a week. In all this he remained an equanimous
and alert figure, with a quick eye for a comic situation and
an impervious patience with children and variously deaf,

obstreperous and indebted customers. When I was about eight, and he would be 45 or 46, my father walked briskly through the house one day when an electrician was doing some wiring up a ladder. The electrician said to my mother 'Is that your eldest?' My father howled with laughter when he was told. It was one of my mother's favourite stories. (My mother died while this book was in preparation.)

There was a period of over-emphatic religiosity in the house. It came at the height of the war, when the Methodists were exhorting their members to extra evangelical fervour, presumably as a contribution to the national resolve. Family Bible reading was apparently urged, and for a while this ritual was observed every night in the living-room. Briefly I enjoyed it because it nourished my conceit over my facility with biblical gob-stoppers. But there developed an embarrassment over this piety. There was something altogether too solemn about it, and it soon became a point of irritation, so was withdrawn from the routine. (I was an enthusiastic Christian, from time to time, around the ages of eight to twelve, gabbling prayers before sleep and butting into adults' talk with impertinent snatches of moral censure that I had picked up from preachers' sermons. I liked the sound of declamation, and must have been irritating. 'We're all sinners,' I would tell people, and ask them: 'Do we *deserve* peace?' My brother shut me up, with: 'You've heard someone say that.')

The ramifications of the outer family were complex. I had uncles and aunts whom I never saw, and who were discussed at length and with jokes and mimicry when other aunts and uncles joined us. There were more distant relatives, grown-up cousins of my mother, whom we saw frequently for a few years and who sent us expensive presents they could not sensibly afford. I still associate these cousins with Christmas trees, because they provided the first one I ever saw decorated by fairy lights. My sister and I were led into a dark room, with hands held over our eyes, there was a tiny click and we saw a magical thing in glinting red, green and silver. Almost immediately afterwards I realized that what was pleasing the adults in the room so much, so that they were cooing at each other, was not the tree but me, because of my goggling response. Children can be coldly observant at the most unlikely moments, while seeming not to be, and this particular instance was memorably instructive to me. I would be no more than six at the time.

The cousins were one of the London branches of the family, bright with laughter, for ever joking elaborately about imminent dooms such as unemployment and being put out of home into the street. It seemed that the main leisure activity in their district was some kind of hide-and-seek game called The Moonlight Flit, which was an hilarious business involving borrowed prams and wheelbarrows. Life consisted mostly of giggling, cups of tea, faggots and fish and chips when we were with them. It was fun.

An uncle and aunt, never seen before, came to stay with us, and before they arrived I was warned: 'Now, you're not to laugh.' I went with my father to meet them at Cannock railway station, and knew the moment I spotted the wide, floppy hat and the beaming, distracted manner of the aunt that the week would be one of the best jokes of the year. Auntie walked in a series of urgent scampers and confused recoils, as fears of disaster left behind came to her every ten yards. She was like the White Rabbit: 'What a lovely day.' . . . step along firmly, mustn't hang about . . . 'Oh, my goodness, the gas tap.' . . . step it out, got to get on . . . 'Oh, goodness me, the kettle.' . . . Off we go, lovely afternoon. . . . . 'Oh, gracious me, the back door.' When we reached home there was a comic theatricality in the removal of the cartwheel hat, and selecting a safe resting place for it, where it would not be struck by an opening door or slept in by the cat. The voice trilled. We took her out to tea, and she handled the pot in much the same way that I played with my toy aeroplanes. She dive-bombed the cups and zoomed up and across the table with a beam of satisfaction. She was engagingly unconcerned at her effect on conventional people, who thought her dotty. Later I saw her inadequately impersonated in films by Margaret Rutherford. My sister went to stay with her for a while, and regarded her affectionately ever afterwards. Auntie was fond of ice-cream and ginger beer.

I had two uncles who were hairdressers, another who was an accountant, another who was a crack rifle shot and a much-sought judge for amateur boxing tournaments (and who took me to his sports club and gave me a pint of shandy when I was thirteen, which made him faultless in my eyes), another who was a farmer. All these relatives were sufficiently exotic against the obsessive mining background of Blackfords to boast of to my friends occasionally. One possessed uncles, cousins, grandparents in the same way as prize marbles with coloured insides. One could not, of course, swop them in the same way, but they could be listed in ascending order of rarity as points of status. I was totally defeated, stopped dead in mid-flow, while playing this game once, when the opponent I had challenged pointed to a boy four or five years younger than himself, and said casually: 'He's my uncle.' I could not match that.

Some unforgettable lines from family and relations:
An aunt from the south — 'Only the lowest of the low would work down a mine.'
Another aunt — 'And the carpenter looked straight at him and said, "Mister. Bugs and spats don't mix."'
My mother — 'I can account for every penny I spend.'
An uncle — 'The only good Jerry is a dead Jerry. Cold steel.'

My brother – 'It isn't wicked to use the *Methodist Recorder* in the lavatory, is it?'

An aunt, on verbal impropriety among fellow workers in a munitions factory – 'So I said, "If it isn't filth, why does it have to be passed round in an envelope?" '

Another aunt, on a girl's association with foreign servicemen – 'And she says she's doing it for the war effort.'

An uncle, beginning a letter to my parents – 'Once again it is Christmas, and I am provoked to write.'

My mother – 'Gloves are a mark of a gentleman.'

A cousin, staring at a new piggery owned by my father's boss – 'It's disgusting. It's better than *people* live in.'

My father, creating hysterics round the tea table – 'Another cup of tea. Yours faithfully, me.'

My mother – 'I wasn't rude, but I gave him one of my looks.'

The first book to impress me was roughly twice the size of my chest. I was then, at a guess, aged five. It had stiff, shiny covers with needle-sharp corners, and contained pictorial horror-stories. They concerned small animals, and big animals, and they were parables whose message was that small creatures had to do as they were told, otherwise they got beaten or eaten or, at the very least, chased through dark woods whose trees were in league with the big creatures and tripped the small ones up as they ran or swiped them with branches from behind. This book frightened me, but I guarded it like treasure. After a while I stopped being afraid of all the episodes except for the one involving the chase. There was a special power in the drawing of the black roots and tendrils and the terror in the face of the animal/child running away. I ran in my dreams. Shapes, vague and face-less, converged on me. I would wake just as they were about to touch me.

Our house had a lot of books. Two bookcases with glass fronts were full of them, and there were more on shelves and windowsills and on top of chests of drawers. There was a complete Dickens library. R. L. Stevenson, Hugh Walpole and Sir Walter Scott were strongly represented. There were many religious titles, including instructional manuals for preachers. I remember reading few of the books we owned; but I read some of them many times. I was addicted to Robin Hood and King Arthur's knights from infancy to early adolescence. Both sets of characters attracted me before Richmal Crompton's William and his friends, and outlasted them easily. (All three are about gangs, of course.) Arthur Mee's English propaganda for patriotic English children bored me. My sister and her friends listened in weepy thrall to my mother's frequent reading of a Victorian novel called *Oliver and the Twins*, but I found it unbearable, not because of its sentimentality, which actually attracted me, but because it made me blush, and that could not be forgiven.

From the age of ten, possibly a few months earlier, I was a weekly regular at the public library a good mile from home. It was a rectangular wooden building, with an inviting smell of warm dust, and it was run by two teachers, brother and sister, one of whom taught me in the primary school and the other at the infants'. I began with Richmal Crompton and ended (some time around the occasion of my first shaves) with Stephen Leacock, Somerset Maugham and D. H. Lawrence. In between came every book the place had which dealt with English archers, Spanish swordsmen, cowboys (repetitively, Buffalo Bill), and the English public school. The school stories were particularly absorbing. They were accounts of a world quite foreign to my own. Their characters spoke an English never heard, in which a boy had a *pater* and a *chum* and concealed things in a *tuckbox* and played *fives* and was required to keep *cave* in a *dorm* and be caned on the bottom by other boys. This extraordinary state of affairs, definitively described by Talbot Baines Reed, contained twisted chivalry by which young gentlemen were permitted to kick members of the lower orders of their own age, when cornered out of bounds in the town, but not older young gentlemen when assaulted by them. Informing on smokers and fellows seen talking to girls was proper, after a brief searching of conscience, but appealing to authority against bullies was not. One of the reasons why I read so much of this monstrous material was simply that the children's section of the library was heavily stocked with it. Another was that it exerted an undoubtedly potent appeal. The plots mostly concentrated on boys' rivalry for athletic heroes' friendship, but it was not until many years later that I learned I had devoted so many hours to reading homosexual love stories, substantially decorated with sado-masochism and strictures on the God-given superiority of people born with wealth. I have been deeply grateful to the interspersion of those West Country bowmen and Castilian sword fighters in my childhood reading.

I do not remember reading any stories, as a child, about people whose circumstances bore connection with my own. My comics entertained me, like my books, mostly with costume melodrama and boarding school romance, although they drew a little closer to reality with tales about the officer class in the first and second world wars. Against this stuff Miss Crompton's William was very nearly recognizable as flesh and blood, since he went to the pictures and had a pea-shooter; but he lived in a large house in the country, knew what a picnic hamper was, and encountered chauffeurs in uniform.

But I used to read to exhaustion. My father's armchair was the favourite aid to concentration. It was made of heavy wood, with thin arms but thick, loose, bed-like cushions.

The grandfather clock ticked to the slow time of the Spanish galleon oars; the fire, framed in the brass fender, tortured my ankles as the Red Indians lit up the pony express rider; Bing Crosby sang out of his brown box by my left ear as Mainwaring Major led school house into a chorus of Up, Chums, for Chertsey. My parents fretted mildly about the comics, but never questioned the books. They took the *Children's Newspaper* with confidence, but Mr Mee's reputation for tedious niceness put it beyond consideration, as far as I was concerned.

Books were faultless presents among us. I remember buying my father one for Christmas, when I was around eleven (and, of course, using money my parents had given me for present-buying). I looked for one about preaching, and based selection on its size, since I could only afford the slimmest; I never knew its content value, if any. I also remember going to another boy's birthday party, being given a small parcel by my mother to take along as a present to him, and being astonished at his response when he opened up the paper and found a book. He was literally struck dumb for a few seconds by the discovery. It was a book of adventure stories, with a picture of some kind of fight on the jacket – a fur trapper grappling with a wolf, or something of the sort. The boy stared at the picture, turned the book over and found a list of other books on that side, then looked up and said something very like (I am not exaggerating this incident): 'A book! A book! Boy, a book!' He sat down and began reading, and barely lifted his nose all the time the rest of us were there.

I realized, when I began to look around in the house, that there were no other books on the premises. I then realized, with wonder, that this was probably the first time the boy had ever handled a book of his own; that the only books he knew were those he used at school and the hymn-book and

Bible put into his hand when he occasionally went to Sunday school. He was a miner's son, and lived in one of the terrace rows. He had no difficulty with words. There were comics, and film magazines, including a number of thick, American ones, in the house. (I was so fascinated by these, which were quite new to me, that I was still reading them long after the party had broken up and was collected in the night and rain by my father.) But to John a book for personal possession was an improbable thing.

I learned in time that absence of books from the home was commonplace. But the incident had considerable impact on me then. I do not think I drew any implications about deprivation from it. John's general turn-out was noticeably of better quality than many others' in the age-group; his father was almost certainly better paid than mine. But it was one of those vivid indications of difference in everyday assumption that can instruct a child, or a man, about the individuality of people. I had always regarded home and books as natural inseparables; had never imagined the possibility of a home without books. Yet here was someone of my own age, who spoke my slang, played my games, ate my food, who had never connected the two. So I drew no conclusions about advantage and disadvantage; but I certainly noted difference, and of a major kind.

We were a thinking family. A lot of life went on in our heads. In spite of the abundant physical activity in my parents' work and their children's play we were not fully expressed in what we did; what we spoke aloud was a good deal less than the total of what was in our minds. This did not seem to be the case with many families around us, whose responses were more violent, more voluble, more predictable, in trivial issues as well as in important ones. Mothers screamed at their children and at other adults without consideration, without inhibition, and were in turn screamed at.

Tears, blows and quick reconciliation, with much hugging and kissing, were habitual, like eating. It was not so in our house. We were not demonstrative. Because we were talkers it was a major sanction to withdraw conversation. My attachment to words gave me a head teeming with them when my appearance suggested a blank sulk. Conflict in our house was expressed in muteness. Perhaps this was not 'good' for any of us. But it was our way, our style. We were a book-lined family; brooders. Out of this introspection – a condition I have always accepted for myself; I have never understood the common guilt and discomfort about it – could sometimes come some very valuable questions and some insightful answers. 'When do you know you love someone?' my sister, when aged about eleven, asked my mother out of a long silence. 'When you can wash their dirty, snotty handkerchiefs,' my mother replied. I ought to add, to keep faith with my reflectiveness, that my sister was always the most spontaneous of us.

I was going to Birmingham with my mother. I wore my green tweed suit, and the leg-ends of the shorts scratched just above the knees. My shoes shone. My leatherette bala-clava helmet, which I loved dearly because it had muffs to keep the frost out of my over-sized ears, was beginning to fray and was not really big enough for me any more. It could no longer look after the lobes of my ears.

Going to Birmingham was an unusual and important matter. We went when there was special shopping to do. We were going to select the books for the Sunday school prize-giving. The prizes were graded for those with their attendance cards covered in blue-ink stars, down to those with a respectable scattering. Those with hardly any stars, like John who had the American comics, would get nothing. Hard luck. We went on the train.

It was cold and wet. The train had no corridor so no toilets. I wrote my initials, very tall, then very tiny, in the slimy, grey haze on the windows. To open the window in the door you had to pull with all your might at the broad leather strap that dangled down. Then you let go, and the window crashed down inside the bottom half of the door, like the guillotine in the French revolution, and chopped off the workman's head as he bent down on the track to clang the wheels with his hammer. I got him going to Birmingham, but not coming back.

There was a woman in our compartment, heavy and well wrapped up, and she talked most of the way in a refined and deep voice. She talked about death. Her father was dead, her husband was dead, her brothers were dead, her friends were dead. It was the war. Everyone was dead. My mother nodded attentively, and said: 'Oh dear.' It was the air raids, the woman said. Life was very insecure. She had stopped thinking about it. She smiled brightly at me, and I smiled back, and she said: 'Just think, Arthur. We might never get out of this train alive.' My mother said: 'Oh dear.' It was a cheek, I thought, calling me by my name out of the blue like that. She must have heard my mother say it.

Birmingham was wet and gloomy, and full of people in wet and gloomy clothes. Lights shone in faint orange behind windows covered in slimy, grey haze, like the train's. The people were all in a great hurry, with angry faces poking out of scarves up to their chins. My mother and I hurried as well. I looked as angry as I could. My green trousers scratched.

In the bookshop people were not so angry. There was a thin man in glasses who called my mother 'Madam', and a plump woman all in wool who called me 'Lovey'. There were books up to the ceiling. The woman breathed hard when she went up the ladder. First prizes were thick books. Third prizes were as thin as slates.

I was not allowed to select my own first prize. None of the other children could, except the ones who wanted Bibles, and there had to be fairness in all things. My mother wrote down titles, and ticked off names on her list. We went down a steep staircase to the basement, where you bumped into people when you bent down to look at the books on the bottom shelves, then upstairs again, then down, then up. I sat on a chair and read a book. My mother put her right forefinger to her lips and looked at the floor, which meant she was thinking. Was Madam finished? The man was talking over his shoulder, always undecided between one customer and another. Not quite, thank you. 'Are you sleepy, Lovey?' Not quite, thank you.

We went home in the dark; dark all the way from the shop. This time the train was packed. It was full of men and women and big girls, all with oily smudges on the sides of their noses, and trousers smelling of oil, and haversacks smelling of stale bread and oil. The girls had harsh laughs, which smelled of oil. There were people standing in the space between the facing seats, holding the edges of the luggage racks. Between my mother and a man I could see my chest and my kneecaps and I was about two inches wide where their clothes did not spill over me. All the books would come in big parcels on a railway van in about two weeks' time. What would I get?

The train stopped every four or five minutes. The girls shrieked. Voices on the station platforms were the voices of dreams, without faces, always indistinct, coming out of rings of dark air. I went to sleep and woke up with a stomach ache. It went away at our station.

I made a big event of our entrance through the back door. 'We were lucky to get off the train alive,' I said. I had sugar sandwiches for tea.

*   *   *

I went with my mother and my brother to a hundred years ago. We went on a train and a bus to stay with Mrs Hunt at Guiting, in Gloucestershire, where my brother was a baby.

It was a hundred years ago because the house was lit by tall, onion-bottomed lamps with paraffin wicks, and the lavatory was a hole in a bench inside a little shed at the end of the garden path. I was taken for a ride in a pony trap. I slept on a couch on the upstairs landing, except for one night in someone else's house when I slept in a bed as tall as my shoulders, and with humps and valleys as if landscaped. I went for a walk across fields by myself, and was followed home by a foxhound, which made me proud.

Huntsmen and wood fires. Water from a pump. Bats in and out of the windows. No chains to pull. It was a hundred years ago, when David Copperfield ran behind the coaches from London to Dover, and where my brother was a baby.

I was frightened by a bee as big as a bird.

My sister could carry me, when I would allow it, until I was getting on for seven. My brother could run with me on his shoulders until I was about ten. He went to work in the wages office at one of the pits when he was fourteen, about which time he could make an impressively rude noise by fitting his right hand into his left armpit and pumping the left arm violently. He performed this trick for me when he undressed to go to bed, and I giggled myself to sleep over it.

The family always called my sister 'Margaret'. Everyone else called her 'Marg'. We called my brother 'Richard'. Everyone else called him 'Dick'.

My sister had a lot of friends, who talked endlessly about their teachers, about which girls told lies and about whose hairstyles were too old for them. Sometimes I was with my sister and her friends, as they sat about our living-room or someone's back garden, contemptuous of their conversation but refusing to leave, mostly because they told me to. One of these big girls said to me once: 'I'm in love with your brother. He thinks I'm dirt.'

My brother was using Brylcreem. I had long, fine hair, and I woke up one morning with it stuck together in clusters by chewing gum.

When I got my first pair of football boots, after school one day, I put them on in the house, lacing the high ankles tight, and timed things so that I was kicking a ball in the front garden when my brother arrived home from work. He said: 'Who told you to lace them like that? Your Auntie Winnie?'

Sometimes I stole money from him when he left it on the chest of drawers — pennies and ha'pennies. He did not know, or pretended not to.

He grew grave when he joined the Air Training Corps, wearing a blue uniform and a wide beret. He and a friend spent hours in silence in our cold front room, drawing English and German aeroplanes. He did not like the commanding officer, who was a rich shopkeeper, because he addressed the assembled ranks as 'Gentlemen', which my brother said was sarcastic.

A boy my brother's age promoted a fight between me and one of my friends on the recreation field. The youth kept saying to me: 'You'll thrape his ears for him, won't you? Won't you? You'll thrape his ears?' I followed the instruction precisely, aiming exclusively for the ears and scoring many hits. The other boy fought with one fist alternately, holding the other to a red ear. I sensed I was doing well. My brother was informed and stepped between us, laughing, and the fight was over. Later I fought the same boy again, but he was too full of revenge for me. He was naturally tougher, and I ran, remaining frightened of him ever afterwards. We were not a fighting family.

My brother went into the Royal Air Force, and the house seemed half-empty. Soon I felt much older.

7

Scholar

I had to pass the scholarship, and go to grammar school. If I did not pass, who knew what might become of me? I might be down the pit, or doing a milk round. I expected to pass, and so did Billy Pugh. He and I jockeyed each other in top and second places in our class at primary school. Our teacher, the tall and bicycling Miss Crockett, told us she wanted to be proud of us both. We were quick-witted as cash registers, and she rang up mental arithmetic problems on us with a frown and a flourish. She read our essays to the class. They were called 'compositions'.

But my parents had to be certain about my future. My brother, who had not gone to grammar school, had been sent in the evenings for extra compensatory tuition from Mr Parton to improve his chances in life, and now I was sent to Mr Parton as well. Nothing was to be left to chance.

Mr Parton kept a private day school: a big house with an overgrown garden in a road of posh houses. It was one of the roads we went along when we undertook the formal leisure activity of 'going for a walk'. It was a Sunday afternoon road, with trimmed hedges, and trees in front of leaded windows. My father's employer lived there, and he had a fish pond with ornamental rocks and pot animals in and around it. I had played in that garden several times, with the grandsons of the house, and had also lived in the house for a fortnight or so when very small, because my mother was seriously ill. They had been kind to me there, or had tried to be; I was fussed over a good deal, but was always uneasy and never knew which room to be in at what time. There were two sitting-rooms, two maids, a telephone, a big car and a small car. I never admitted to any unhappiness there, because I fully understood that it was not anybody's fault; but I was troubled by the feeling of displacement, and by having no idea how long this removal from the family would last. I retained little detail of my stay there; perhaps I afterwards put it deliberately out of my mind. I remember that my father's employer told me his dad used to thrash him with a dog whip, which conjured pictures to dry my mouth, although I could not give an exact form to the weapon. There was a definite aura of violence about this man, which I sensed behind the chuckles. He mentioned the dog whip several times, when he would say: 'Oh yes, it was always Sam who got it.' I affected an air of unconcern, and waited.

Now I was making regular visits to the road of the posh houses, to be crammed in spelling and sums by Mr Parton, I think twice a week. His house was old and chill. He was old and stooping, and had an habitual cough, faint and high pitched. I was ready for the cough, because my brother had told me about it. You heard the cough before he opened the door.

Sometimes he gave me my lessons in his study, which was a big room at the front of the house, with heavy curtains smelling of mould and with dilapidated armchairs and holes in the carpet. He had far more books than even we had at home. I preferred being in this room, because it was unlike being at school. But it was as cold as an air raid shelter.

He was a gentle, nervous old man, and I could see that he was in a poor way physically and financially. The text books I worked from there were like sponges with use, the lettering on their covers barely readable. He seemed to be dealing with more than one private pupil at a time, because he would set me an exercise and then hurry off to some other part of the house. I would hear voices as doors opened and shut; his cough would rap in the corridor; I would get my head down over my book and write in the laborious, individual lettering that the primary school insisted on. Cough, cough, cough. 'Now, how are *you* getting along, young man?' Cough, cough. 'I see. What's your name?' He told my mother: 'Your little boy can't write.'

He had a conventional schoolroom, where his day children sat, and it had the correct classroom smell of chalk, milk and damp clothes. I disliked having my lessons in there. He sat at his desk in front of the blackboard, and in the evening gloom it was like being kept in.

We were very polite to each other. He never shouted or gave a hint of ill-temper, and I used to wonder whether such an unlikely atmosphere for a classroom existed also during the day. He said 'please' in the genuine way, not as the word was used by the teachers in my own school, when it was a steely reinforcement of instruction or warning.

Mr Parton had a grown up son, who took my lessons occasionally. He was long and thin to the point of frailty, as if he could turn round and round inside his clothes while they stayed still facing you. He was just as polite as his father.

But I was always relieved when the lessons were over. The house was glum with decay and tiredness. It gave me a peculiar feeling that I had gone very pale and weak. I cannot remember how many months I went to the Partons for these lessons, but I associate them exclusively with November.

It is nearly dark when I reach the house, the spooky garden is dripping wet after rain, and I take a deep breath as I walk into the classroom, where an old man is fixing the blackout curtaining; and the seat of the desk is cold-damp against the backs of my knees, and I shrink to half my size in the room's damp pallor. 'Now, young man. What's your name?'

School became tense. Miss Crockett was seen to hurry. We were close to the scholarship day. We got tongue-tied.

Miss Crockett gave us a round of rapid question-and-answer, and called everyone who failed out to the front to be caned. In the end she had half the class standing in a line from wall to wall, including Billy Pugh and me. She was in a dither. She walked along the line, tapping each held-out hand nervously with her stick. Billy was last. He said to her: 'My dad says I haven't got to hold my hand out for the cane, Miss.' Miss Crockett looked as if she was going to faint. She looked along the line, and said: 'Well, Billy, really. You've let me get this far.' Then she looked along the line again, and said: 'Well, it was only a tap, wasn't it?' She was distressed. We were delighted.

We took forms home to be filled in. Our parents had to name the grammar school they wanted us to go to, if we passed the examination. I was entered for one about twelve miles away, because the older of two brothers I was friendly with was already there; their father was a teacher somewhere else. Billy was entered for another which was nearer. On the day of the examination I felt extremely important, and as brilliant as a B.A. Nervousness was lost in impatience.

We sat in long lines in the primary school hall. There were an English paper and an arithmetic paper, and neither gave me any trouble. Billy said the same thing afterwards. We felt very close friends, although we seldom saw each other outside school. We both knew we had passed that part of the examination, and we were right. The next part was called The Intelligence Test. I was taken to the grammar school on a bus, and joined a long file into the school hall.

At that point I knew I was on the threshold of a new world. The hall was grand, domed, churchlike, and I found I was among the largest number of boys I had ever seen collected in one place. They had all passed their English and arithmetic papers, and I was alarmed by the implied severity of the competition. The paper was like nothing I had ever associated with school work. It appeared more like a compendium of verbal tricks of the 'Adam and Eve and Pinch Me . . .' kind. The first question said simply: 'Put a dot in this circle.' I was intensely suspicious, and pressed home the dot only after a lot of deliberation and flicking sideways glances in the hope that I might see what other people were doing. Masters walked up and down the rows of desks, glowering. 'Put a square in this circle.' There *had* to be something behind all this. 'Which shape is the odd one out?' There *had* to be something I'd missed. I answered all the questions, with gathering disconcertion, was taken home dazed and disbelieving, and was later surprised to hear that I had passed that test as well. Then came something anticipated with dread, its nature only guessed at, and called inscrutably The Oral.

I sat outside the grammar school headmaster's study, beside my father and with roughly a score more boys with parents. We could hear the headmaster's voice booming on the other side of the door, and he sounded twelve feet tall. When it was my turn he was found to be my father's size, and and to have a limp. I read something to him out of a book, using my best speak-up voice borrowed from Sunday school for the occasion, and then answered questions about the extract. The dog had been white; the man had been tall; there were three other men; it was a warm day. . . . My father and the headmaster shook hands, the headmaster called me 'Arthur'. It was the only time he ever did.

Some time afterwards my parents were informed by letter

that I was acceptable to the grammar school they had named, and would they furnish the following details about their income, to determine how much they should pay per term for the privilege? Billy was accepted for the other grammar school, and we never met again. We were the only ones at our school to pass the scholarship that year. Whether Mr Parton's evening lessons, at significant expense to my parents, helped me in this so highly valued success, I can never know. What I certainly knew at the time was that I wished someone had prepared me for the intimidating size of the grammar school hall.

Among my friends there was a boy named Herbert, who did not pass, and his mother said *she* knew what had got me through the scholarship: it was because I delivered Miss Crockett's weekly order of cakes from my father's shop. In time I came to wish with fervent ingratitude to everyone concerned that I had not passed anyway.

Meanwhile, John, who had the American comics, met me in the street and looked me square on in an adult, earnest way, and said: 'You're a scholar.'

I was aged ten years and ten months when I began my first term at grammar school. On the first day I left home at eight a.m. and got aboard the red double-decker bus at 8.20 for the half-hour journey, wearing new clothes all over, with identical cloth badges on the breast pocket of my navy-blue blazer and on my cap, which was pulled square and hot over my forehead so that I had to keep my chin up to see where I was going, and was received with howls of derision by the hardened old lags who had their caps in their pockets. I had a gleaming leather millstone round my neck, called a satchel. There were boys on the bus with voices like Paul Robeson's, and they could jam their heads against the ceiling without as much as lifting their heels. I found the face of the older boy

I already knew, smiled at him and received a sneer of utter contempt. I was dumbly terrified. There were three or four other new caps rammed over white faces, and when we got off the bus we huddled together as we followed the crowd. No-one met us, no-one told us anything. We swam for that first morning, a growing shoal of minnows as other buses arrived from other places, among waves of indifference and arrogance. We were irritably pushed about from one class-room to another until we found ourselves in our proper places. We were 3A, 3B or 3C. I was 3A. The As were the cleverest. I felt as clever as a housebrick.

During the first week the general fear subsided into wariness, and when that went away there were only recurrences of fear at particular times. The man who taught us geography punched boys out of their seats with his clenched fists. He punched in the back, producing tears and nausea. This was part of his normal teaching method throughout the lower and middle school, and he appeared to require at least one out-burst of sobbing to a lesson. There were often several. The man who taught us French slapped boys across the face and ear with his open hand, although his assaults were less frequent than the geography teacher's. The man who taught us history bored a bunch of keys into the backs of heads and necks.

An explanation for some of this improvised physical punishment was eventually suggested one day by the history master. Infuriated by some boy's reply to a question, he stared for a long time at him while the silence grew into a barely tolerable air-compression around us. Then he said slowly to the boy: 'I wish we'd got Old Crip back.' (Old Crip was the nickname for a pre-war headmaster, who re-appeared violently but not for long among us, during which time his study was associated exclusively with beating.) 'I wish we'd got Old Crip back,' the history master repeated,

'I'd have had you over this desk.' He then turned his head slowly round the class, until he was looking at me, and said: 'And you.' We concluded that there had been a time when the cane was used with some ceremony in the classroom, instead of only by the headmaster. Logically, the staff had to find their own substitutes for it.

This was not the case with all of them. We had women teachers from time to time whom my class treated amiably and who were amiable in return. There were a couple of English masters who never struck anyone. The man who took physics managed to cope with our various groupings of the incomprehending, the dangerously experimental and the precocious, in a milling din of activity, without raising a finger in anger. We had a woodwork master who was un-ending in his patience with the helpless, like me. The ones who knocked us about simply chose to. In revenge we selected victims among the staff.

There was an old teacher martyred to arthritis, which particularly affected his hands. He had a victim's name, like Blubberly. On the days when he was obviously close to distraction with pain we abandoned work, played pontoon, tore each other's fly buttons open, wrote out the soccer team that ought to be playing for England, usually containing a minimum of six Wolverhampton Wanderers players, and laughed at him in unison when he tried to resume the lesson. Sometimes he would sit the forty-five minutes out, with his head lolling low. Occasionally he would leave us to it, walking away with his fingers crooked downwards, up near his chest. I never saw him cry. We made another master cry several times.

He was a tiny refugee Jew, quite young. It is fair to assume that he had already suffered some kind of hardship before he reached us, since he was from Central Europe and, according to his accent, had not been many years in Britain.

We gave him no consideration for that. He seemed to be some kind of all-purpose stand-in for the rest of the staff because he took several different subjects for two or three days at a time. I was by now halfway up the school. We would be sitting waiting for him, bolt upright in our desks, all frowning in apparent concentration, and although he would have seen this pretence before, and experienced the abuse that followed it, he would still smile and make his little bow as he walked in. We would let him speak several times, and not answer, to allow the tension to build, and then launch a concerted desk-banging and jeering at him. We would shout rude words, including 'cheap thrill' and 'prostitute', get up and sit on our desk lids with our backs to him, and do impersonations of Crosby. After a while he would start shouting, and would bounce up and down in his chair, and then run about the room, first along one aisle and then another, appealing to individuals with tears in his eyes. He was obviously unable to face any kind of violence, and I cannot remember that he ever reported any of us to the headmaster. The climax to this baiting came when he suffered a form of instant nervous breakdown in front of us. He advanced towards an ingeniously troublesome boy in glasses (the boy was an excellent pianist, who played Chopin dramatically on the stage of the school hall), and after drumming his feet on the floor struck our virtuoso across the face. Then he put both hands over his eyes – we could hear him sobbing – and ran out of the room, and away from us for ever. No-one was punished.

We had an old master, called The Major, who taught languages. He had the kind of moustache that retired majors had in films, short and sparse and yellow at the ends of the bristles from his pipe-smoking, and he called us 'Old Man' and was always shaking hands with us in the street. He tried to entertain us a great deal with stories about cavalry life, which we quickly forgot, and often talked about urinating and the unnecessary privacy attached to it: 'When you're riding a horse, does he bother to duck down behind some hedge or wall when he wants to do his business? No. Good heavens, no. He just gets on with it. There's far too much made of these things.'

We had a much younger ex-military man – or Air Force man? I was never sure – called Algy, who was apparently mad. He enjoyed lessons enormously, maintaining a great toothy grin and bursting out with peels of laughter in an exaggerated country-gentleman tone. He laughed: 'Haw-hah-haw, haw-haw, haw-haw!' He could simulate the crack of small arms fire with a spitting sound, and would crouch behind his desk and hold mock gun-fights with us. I think, although I cannot be sure, that Algy taught us English for a while. He certainly superintended some of our compulsory rugby games, using his unconvincing upper class voice again: 'Don't kick et it, men. Pick the demn thing ap end ran with it.' The Major looked after rugby as well, and knew more about it. He pushed us into the scrums and ran beside us, nudging us on. He was a surprisingly fast runner for his age and could keep pace with a threequarter for quite a distance. Once when I met The Major in the town during the lunch break he lifted me off my feet with both arms and swung me round, shouting, 'Hello, old man, hello.' Every boy was 'Old Man.' The Major seemed not to know anybody's name, however much he liked him.

I was at the school between September 1943 and the end of 1948, so that the war had a strong influence on the composition of the staff for most of my time there. I realized that fact while I was still a boy, and understood its implications more later on. The factor does not diminish the reality of my pitifully inadequate formal education. I arrived at the school with a grasp of classroom work which was certainly above the average, stayed with the leaders for about eighteen months, and then rapidly sank into indolence and a bored resistance. By the time the school was substantially re-staffed with youngish, career teachers I had firmly established a resentment of the place.

It was dated from the Reformation, and there was a distinct fostering of conceit about its age and its imitative public school practices, which became irksome. It had a fee-paying preparatory department, whose products were the ones among us with the cricket whites, freshly laundered, and whose conversation with some of the staff showed that their fathers knew the masters socially. Several of these teachers were much amused by the coarse accents of some of the boys who came in from the surrounding districts with torn pockets and talk about paper rounds and potato-picking and fights in pubs. Before I left my parents had stopped having to pay fees determined by means, and the coarse accents were more than holding their own in number and volume against the other kind; but I never lost the awareness of a division. I did not feel any discrimination, but I was conscious of having unwanted identification marks of 'superiority' imposed on me. Grievously, we had to play rugby, like the public schools whose peculiar way of life I had examined through the prose of Mr Talbot Baines Reed, in spite of the obsession so many of us had with *real* football since infancy. We were surrounded by soccer clubs which were glamorous to us – Wolves, Stoke City, Aston Villa, Derby County – and we played the game intuitively in most of our spare time. But the school insisted on rugby, whose *tone* was different along with the ball and the rules, and in that way stubbornly excluded us. I once ran into a parti-cularly heavy thump in the face in a rugby game, to which I was giving my usual, sullen half-interest, and the master in charge of the match shouted to the thumper: 'Well done.

I've been wanting to do that for days.' I was not surprised, although I was not aware that I had given this teacher any great annoyance; life by now was an accepted state of hostility. Most lessons had become tedious mysteries; the teachers applied themselves to the minds of the gifted and the interested in the front seats and let the rest of us yawn and admire each other's erections.

With the painful indecision of early adolescence I was never certain whether I properly belonged among the lumpen disregarded or the brazen rebellious. I was bored by the one camp and too timid for full acceptance by the other, and moved miserably between the two. I withdrew so much for a while that I could often fail completely to understand what was being said to me, even though I could hear it plainly. This applied equally to teachers with precise enunciation and to old friends of primary school days when I met them in the street around my home. I stopped playing football on the recreation field, stared blankly at homework, refused to continue going to Sunday school or to piano lessons, and consoled myself with reading and with the absorbing pleasure of combing my hair. Frequently I missed the bus to school, deliberately, so that I could travel alone on the next one, and then crept into the building to hide in the cloakroom during morning assembly. Much of the period between the ages of about thirteen-and-a-half towards fifteen was achingly unhappy for me. The intense stomach pains and vomiting which had plagued me before infants school now returned, sometimes sending me home with mixed shame and relief in the middle of afternoon classes. By Thursday morning I had built up a nauseous despondency, which vanished instantly in the brilliant refreshment of walking out of school on Friday afternoon with a weekend of freedom before me. (I write 'brilliant' because the feeling as I walked through that door was as if a very bright light settled around me.) And I would go to bed on Sunday night with the familiar, sickening, dull weight climbing back on to my shoulders.

I ended one bleak term at the bottom of the class, with a column of 'D' ratings on my report form and appropriately abusive comments from every teacher except the one who taught us English. I had written an essay that term in which I had described in detail the interior of my father's shop, and it had plainly surprised the English teacher. He asked me repeatedly: 'Who helped you with this?' My parents read the report as if going through an account of a disaster at one of the local pits, and then threw it on the fire. I stared at the flames and saw the face of the mathematics master, with its black moustache, burning on the end of a window pole.

The confusions of puberty (as one understands only a long time later) must have had much to do with this misery, this prolonged sulking of the intellect. Ambiguity was everywhere. In the last two terms before the School Certificate year I was in a class which contained boys who were still childlike, in short trousers and with model aeroplanes under their arms, and also youths with incipient beards and possessed of obsessive detail on film stars, swing bands and girls' bodies; and between these two groups there was no more than a year in age. Because it was an all-boys school our sexual impulsion was inevitably much exercised, and fostered, among each other. Mostly it was satisfied in violent horseplay; there was an extremely popular, and forbidden, game called 'frigging', which involved a wrestling match whose object was to see which of the contestants could expose the other's privates. More impressively one boy might boast that he had sat through an entire lesson with his hand inside his own or another's flies. We were not always at individual desks.

We knew what all this was about, because there were

frequent discussions concerning who was 'over-sexed' and who was 'under-sexed', and who, indeed, was 'a sex maniac'. But if there were close, personal relationships of a more truly homosexual nature I did not observe any, although there were one or two pairs of friends who were suspected. It was recognized that an accusation of such a serious, secretive involvement was too damaging to be made directly without proof. What these boys did together was mysterious, and not the issue; it was the privacy that offended. I recall that I was at one time greatly attracted by a much younger boy with black curls and a quick, round figure, and used to watch him a lot as he ran about in the lunch hour; but I never thought to seek any contact. There was a general atmosphere of leering loutishness. It was before the days of sex instruction in schools; the biology lessons skirted all round the subject, with a guided tour of tibias, fibulas, clavicles, rib-cages, but never entered the controversy, or even its physical area.

Girls arrived on the school bus; that is, they were suddenly noticed. Their High School was a quarter of a mile from ours. The bus became a transport of discovery. Joyce sat on my knees, heavier than I was, plump and exciting to the touch. The girls heaved under their blouses, blushed in their squeals and gave us sweets. The conversation was suggestive, perilous. Was I fast? Was she easy? Did I know that So-and-so was hell for a girl to keep under control? Did she know that So-and-so might not be the only one? We arranged to go to the pictures, and met outside. 'Here's Jean and Brian,' she said, and she and Jean looked at each other in unmistakable conspiracy. 'Are you going upstairs or downstairs?' I said to Brian. 'Down,' he said. 'Right, we're going up,' I said, and my lover and I managed to find the money between us. 'I didn't know they were coming', she said, lying. 'Hmm,' I said, feeling deceived and sophisticated because of it. We held hands and I got one arm round her thick shoulders, just. We leaned our heads together, and trembled, and didn't kiss. I smoked a cigarette, though.

I grew up, bang, and was a boy again, bang. One Sunday evening I sang The Lord's My Shepherd to the tune of Crimond as a solo at an evening service conducted by my father, my voice still treble although roughening, some time approaching my fourteenth birthday. Very soon afterwards I was going to my sister's youth club, saying I was fifteen and kissing factory girls in the dark. We sat round one of the small rooms in twos, and when the lights went out we kissed. When the lights went on again we stopped kissing and chatted. When the lights went out we kissed again.

We played table tennis and kissing. There were all kinds of kissing: wet, dry, French, when the tongue was fluttered, in particular. There was an elaborate, daring kind when, standing up with all the lights on and people watching, you bent the girl backwards and sideways so that she hung hazardously from your powerful arms. Since I was not as big as half the girls I had few opportunities for this; but I much admired the performances of some of the older members with gruff voices from the waggon sheds. I was embarrassed by the white delicacy of my hands against the weight and scarred masculinity of these young men's, but I took great pleasure in acceptance by this adult company. We sat round the stove, and I listened to long, circumstantial accounts of rape. (They owed a lot to the *News of the World*, as I later realized, because of the recurrent incidence of the phrase, 'Sexual intercourse then took place.') We played records by Glenn Miller, Tommy Dorsey, Woody Herman, Harry James. It was American music, and America was the ultimate glamour. I felt twenty and sensual, and school was preposterously irrelevant. When asked what my job was I would say, 'Student,' and change the subject.

Hunched one morning at the bus stop, having missed the eight-twenty again, I heard a voice of that special universal womanliness which is the mother in the breast, and it said: 'Isn't he lovely, Nance?' I turned and looked at two working girls in their late teens, who looked frankly back and then giggled and linked arms. There was an age between us. Going to school, I was still a child.

The war had long ended by now, the world's release from its murder having made little impact on me in my preoccupation with growing. Towards the end of it I had been intrigued by the presence among us of American Negro soldiers, being aware of a mixture of pity and fear with which they were regarded in the community. Odd comments had registered and lingered, such as, 'Their hearts are as white as ours,' and 'They're very fond of children, you know'; and there were stories about a fight between them and a group of white soldiers, in which knives had been used; and a neighbour's daughter had married one. I had slept through V.E. Night, and only knew the next morning that people had danced for hours in the street in the centre of the town. The grisly revelations about Belsen and Buchenwald had not prompted much comment in my age group. It was as if we had simply outgrown the war, like the marbles phase and our vulnerability to bullying. It had been part of smallness and cold knees. Grammar school lessons ignored it; our studies of history were not to advance beyond the French revolution. The war was our background, more conditioning than we knew but of minor immediate interest.

My sister was now at work in a chemist's shop, lost to me in the mysteries of cosmetics and home-perms. My brother reappeared on leave from time to time, bored with office work now that he was not going to be an air-gunner after all, and I picked up attractive bits of Air Force slang from him including, 'Press on, redundant', and, 'Look after Number One'. I trotted them out to no good effect until I tired of them.

I rejected the idea of going camping with the school as a project too childish to contemplate, but was intensely excited by the proposition of a week in the Lake District. We were given a list of necessary equipment, and I answered a newspaper advertisement for reconditioned Army boots and surplus socks, acquired an RAF battledress jacket, and rubbed my feet with surgical spirit to harden them for tramping. I had never before seen a mountain.

It turned out to be a deeply influential week, because although the presence of teachers and their orders reduced the enjoyment below my hopes I experienced an instantaneous thrill and sense of rapport on contact with this particular environment; and in later years I was to be grateful for that introduction to mountaineering. Catbells was my first hill, and even in its modest size and gradient it spoke to me in a private and telling way, touching the inner being as some literature and some music can. I said nothing of that kind at the time, naturally, showing much more interest in the dance we went to on the Saturday night, eyeing girls with unfamiliar accents, and joining in the grumbling about youth hostel food and rain down the neck; but I was well aware of having come across something important to me. The mathematics master was there, just as gloomy and just as intractable in conversation as ever; but I was less unnerved by him afterwards. If his subject remained impenetrable to me he was seen to have a life outside it. Until then he was as inseparable from a logarithm as if he was one, and nothing else in life was as malevolent. (I look up 'logarithm' in my dictionary now, and I read: 'the index of the power to which a fixed number or base must be raised to produce the number'. The puzzle is not that I should never have been

able to comprehend this as a boy, nor that I cannot comprehend it now, but that anyone should imagine I might. To
me it is utterly opaque. I suppose the point is that I always
expected mathematics to be explicable in words, and never
grasped the fact that number was quite a different kind of
'sense'. It has really been of no help when mathematics has
been described to me as a different 'language', because
language can be translated word-to-word. Mathematics
means nothing but itself. My mistake, which no-one ever
managed to correct, possibly because it was not perceived,
was that I thought that its symbols *were* symbols, in the
literary sense. I still do not understand, but do not expect
to.)

Perhaps the trip to the Lake District enabled the school
to 'get through' to me, to use one of the popular terms in
education nowadays. Perhaps it merely coincided with the
natural resolving of alarms and bewilderments that the
passing of a few months can effect in youth. Certainly
tensions eased around this time. The solemn call of duty was
manifest in the irrefutable necessity of passing the School
Certificate examination, and to this awesome task I applied
what mental agility I could re-summon. In at least half the
subjects I was no less bemused than before; I simply learned
my lines.

It was a help that there was now a lighter, more relaxed
air about the corridors. We had several visibly young teachers,
improbably with full heads of hair and cheerful attitudes;
at least one of them used to whistle pop songs; another told
us he was a Socialist; a third played a fluent Fats Waller type
of piano, and was noticed by one of my friends among the
crowd at all-in wrestling matches. A measure of reciprocal
respect settled on us. I asked the new headmaster what the
difference was between the aims and objects of Christianity
and communism, and he gave me a long, careful answer

centring on the rights of the individual in society. I wrote
an essay in celebration of Katherine Hepburn's face, which
involved me in a dispute with the new English master on
whether her eyes were fractionally too close together to
qualify her for the accepted use of the word 'beautiful'. I
said they were; he said not. It was important.

I had known since I was around thirteen that I would
become a journalist, that I would leave school to begin work
without considering the possibility of university, which was
only for the very brilliant or the rich, and that I would travel
the world on a magic carpet of words and dramatic en-
counter. Now that my translation to this happy condition was
drawing near – that is, I was in my last year at school; I had
no idea at all how I was to get a job – there was a growing
optimism in my life. The future was worth working for; or,
at any rate, waiting for.

The examination was as mystifying as it was expected to
be, and I laboured through it with no conviction but with
a sacrificial patience, and afterwards congratulated myself
that I could not be expected to do another day's work as long
as I was in the school. (I was proved right.)

But I was not prepared for the conversation I had with
one of the masters shortly before the end of the term. He
said: 'I believe you want to be a journalist?' I said I did. He
said that the owner of one of the weekly newspapers in the
district was a friend of his, and then added: 'He'll have a
vacancy later this year for a junior reporter. Do you want to
go and see him?' I was amazed to find, as was obvious, that
some lobbying on my behalf had been done by a man who had
always seemed at best exasperated by me; I never expected
any kind of assistance from him, and this was an unimagined
service. I went to the interview with my heart deafening my
thoughts like a gong of gold. I wore my yellow string gloves.

The office was in a side street. The firm did jobbing

printing along with publishing its weekly paper, and the building clattered in a smell of ink, glue, gas fires, and linoleum on the point of ignition. There were bicycles in its passages and spilled tea on the stairs. The proprietor was my mother's vision of a gentleman, in a discreet suit and with a bold forehead and a firm, pleasant voice. I was 'Mr Hopcraft' in his first sentence, and 'Arthur' afterwards. He called in the editor, who looked less relaxed, biting on a pipe and with purple eyes in a grey head, and they asked me friendly questions about my father's work and what books I had read. They said I could have the job, when it became vacant in the new year; I would then be sixteen. It was still summer, so the delay would give me time to learn some rudimentary shorthand. Pay was to be decided in a confirmatory interview with one of my parents. We shook hands, and I replaced the unnecessary yellow glove on to my right hand and fitted the other glove stylishly between right thumb and forefinger, placing my left hand into left trouser pocket, also stylishly. The editor gave a tiny giggle, and said to the proprietor: 'I think he looks like a reporter.' I went down the stairs with a roller skate on one foot and the other stuck in a kettledrum.

It was a mild surprise, then a smug self-justification, to learn that I had actually secured a School Certificate. I had, I think, three Credits and four Passes. I remember that I was awarded only a Pass for English literature, yet a Credit for mathematics, which convinced me of the fortuitous nature of the whole episode as far as my own abilities were concerned. English literature was my one deep interest in school work; but I probably did not treat it sufficiently as a 'subject'. It was more, also, than a pleasure; it was integral in my life, like football. At least I had the document, which made some practical sense of the five years of intermittent

disconsolation and the cost and alarm to my parents. It has
been a sardonic little irony to note that the possession of the
certificate has never had the slightest significance in my life
since, beyond the memory of the pain that getting it created.
I think it is also accurate to say that grammar school did not
educate me, but that its major importance to me lay simply
in the fact that I went there. The scholarship examination I
passed at the age of ten was the one vitally influential factor
of my education; the mystique of qualification that went in
those days with the label 'grammar school boy' overrided my
failure in classes. If I had not passed that examination my
chances of entering journalism would have been much more
slight; it is most unlikely that I would have come into contact
with a teacher who had access to a newspaper owner; I
remain astonished that the man chose to help me, because
even as an adult it is so difficult to adjust one's reading of the
character of a man whom one firmly fixed as hostile when a
child; obviously he had a sympathy and a concern I never
guessed at in my morose resistance. But my image of him,
long and tweedy and hairy-eared, is inseparable from the
blood-red clash of milk bottles that occurred inside my head
whenever he struck me in the face, and the dentist's-chair
numbness that followed it. I hated him, and I am grateful to
him.

I had a single, silly term in the sixth form, waiting to
leave and get to work. I was supposed to be studying
Economic History. I write the words with capital initials
because that is the way I used to speak them – grandly, as if
giving myself a title. I chose the subject, in fact invented its
name. 'I want to do, er, Economic History,' I told the headmaster, believing it sounded the sort of material a future
political correspondent of the *News Chronicle* ought to
know about; and a future foreign correspondent of the *News
Chronicle*, too, if that was the way things might turn out. The

history master found me a suitable book on the fundamentals of political science (I think; its title and author have long ago gone from memory), and left me to read in private pomposity in the library. Once a week, as long as agreeable weather coincided with twenty minutes or so of his available time, he would walk me round the playing field, asking me what I understood democracy to be, or the role of elected representatives. It seemed not a very long time since he had impressed upon me how satisfying he would have found it to beat me over his desk. It was actually about two years.

The cane was still a major presence. During this term I once stood outside the headmaster's study, waiting to see him about a free bus warrant, with a very small boy beside me, summoned for some similar administrative matter, and we suddenly heard the sound of the cane being used on the other side of the door. The child looked up at me, wide-eyed in fear, and then turned as if to run off. I pulled him back, and said: 'It's nothing to do with us.' He was trembling. Soon a boy of his age came out, with his eyes full of tears and a look of white shock all over his face, and saying repeatedly, 'Oh,' in the senseless way that people do when they *are* suffering from shock. I went into the study, and when the headmaster had taken, or given, the necessary information he said: 'Send that wretched boy in here, will you?' I thought he meant the tiny, terrified one, who was, after all, going to be caned, and I was troubled immediately by a mixed feeling of injustice and frightened, protective responsibility. I said: 'Which one, sir?' The headmaster was smiling in tolerant, easy patience. 'That wretched little person who came out as you came in,' he said. His description was more true than it ought to have been. I felt an intolerable urgency that afternoon to be away from the place.

The only class I attended in these last three months at school was, of course, the English one. We had yet another new teacher, one seemingly fresh out of the army, who was a flamboyant table-tennis player and who remarked casually that the only reason we enjoyed shouting the words 'Fuck' and 'Shit' and 'Cunt' at each other so much was because we had never lived in a barrack room and become utterly tired of their repetition. The adult good sense of this subtle rebuke, as well as the man's calm, informal manner, impressed me greatly; swearing was cut down. He was invaluable in showing the gulf of quality between (and he would list them) Priestley-Maugham-Bennett and D. H. Lawrence, by asking us to compare how much we knew about the characters in the writers' books besides their physical peculiarities. This elementary test in criticism came as a revelation at the time. But I sometimes found this man daunting. I wrote him an essay, whose subject I cannot remember; but I recall what he wrote at the bottom of it. He commented: 'Quite well argued. But you do not really get down to evaluating our society.' I am sure he was right.

He was the only teacher I met at the school whom I actively admired; I told people so. I am unable to remember his name.

I unroll a long, narrow photograph of the assembled school, which is dated May 1947, and which recently emerged from some corner-dusting in my parents' house. I am looking out from the fifth row of eight from the front, and near the left end; I would be fourteen-and-a-half. I have a lot of hair, wavy and ruffled, am wearing a tie between two boys who are not and am offering to the world what I suppose must have passed for my frank, open gaze at the time. We look a more relaxed, amiable lot than I remember; certainly not in the least do we suggest recalcitrance or dismay. We are a little ragged and perhaps also under-weight by 1970 standards, not uniformly dressed even for this official occasion.

The Staff appear mild, and quite the sort of people ready to deal considerately with the disconcertions of the young. How surprising I find that. How false.

I recognize perhaps a fifth of these five hundred faces of my past; and there they belong utterly. I can give names to about twenty. I know for sure the present circumstances of only two of them, brothers: one now teaching in Africa, either East or West I am uncertain; the other is a florist in his home town. One other face was last reported sighted in public relations. I cannot look along these eight rows without some emotion, although not much. They are faces from old conflicts, some passionate and damaging, and all, I suppose, echoed somewhere in my personality. I have no interest in these people's present or their future. It is what they were which is part of me, and I realize now that really I knew little about them. On our photograph we are bland. I know we were not that.

8

Postman's Knock

I ended my last term at school a few days early, and became a Christmas postman. . . .

The morning woke in the night and groped grey and stiff against blackness; grey and stiff people, hedges and lampposts; and footsteps isolated and intent. I had wool round my mouth and ears and setting my nerve ends prickling where they stuck out beyond bitten finger-nails. The air had coke in it. It was an unnerving time of day.

The sorting office was lit yellow, and smelled of dust and sacking, and the sorters worked in their overcoats at the rows of pigeon holes and canvas skips. The postmen were mostly women.

'You one of the temps?'

'Yes.'

'Just write your time of arrival on this card. You want to keep it filled in. Time of arrival, time of going off, morning and afternoon. The longer you work the more you get paid. Get it?'

'Of course.'

'Just hang on a bit till you get allocated.'

I was allocated to one of the women. What was her real name? I nicknamed her Mrs Gandhi. She was small and made of cheesewire beneath her lamination of clothing. The layers progressed in thickness from inner to outer and diminished in length in the same progression: lisle stockings, cotton socks to the calf, woollen ankle socks; cotton dress reaching to the ankle socks, tweed coat to the cotton socks, another tweed coat to the knees, something home-made out of mackintosh and tweed to the waist. She had a pixie hat, like a little girl's, made from a scarf whose ends she tied round the throat. Her eyes were slitty behind round, Gandhi glasses, and fine grey hairs came out of her chin. She was full of rumination and silent plot, smelled rank and had the hands of a navvy. She hardly ever spoke, but jerked the point of her pixie hat at parcels to be picked up and letter bags to be carried and streets to be dealt with.

We would set off together, banging bus stops and people with our bulging bags in the fog, slithering on puddles of ice. She could right herself with the weightless ease of a child. We shared the streets disproportionately. I had the long ones, the ones with flights of steps going up to the front doors, and the one that stretched away among hedges, with menacing, shrouded houses set among piles of scrap and guarded by platoons of geese. She took the short streets, the terraces with access alleys that enabled her to follow a convenient course from one front door to its neighbour's back and so on down the street. This wasn't necessary; she could have covered the street more quickly by keeping to front doors. It was one of her rituals. She had staging posts for cups of tea and nips of stout: steaming back kitchens with scowling old cats watching their fur smoulder against the grate and with BLESS THIS HOUSE in glitter dust on a drawing pin. Her logistics had a rare exactitude, and she never failed to appear on the right corner to join up with me on the return walk to the sorting office. 'You're a good lad,' she would say, and give me biscuits picked up from her regulars. Her voice was tantalizing in that it sounded nearly cultured; but she didn't use it enough for me to be sure.

She seldom referred to people's names, and she had her own terms for houses. 'Clock house', she would say, poking her pixie hat. 'Drains', and poke again. 'Wireless', and another poke. 'Spotted dog.... Bread pudding.... Crutches.'

We had a remarkable variety of the well-to-do, the scruffy, the house-bound and the never-at-home on our route. There was a portly, puffing man who often met us on his way to work as we parted at the corner of his street and he would say with elaborate deference something like: 'I would be deeply obliged if you could allow me to relieve you of my post here.' Every time Mrs Gandhi would reply: 'Illegal.' The man would make tut-tutting noises, and puff away. He was a solicitor.

Mrs Gandhi had a withering way with dogs, which I envied. She sneered at them, pointed her pixie hat, and they retreated, sometimes sideways. The sorting office staff were just as nervous of her.

'Getting on all right?'

'Sure.'

'Funny old bugger, ay 'er?'

'You're telling me.'

'Not trying it on, is 'er?'

'Let her try it, that's all.'

'That's the road, cock. She's a funny old bugger.'

But they treated her carefully. She could whistle carols, with firm top notes. Tuneful whistling is unusual among women.

By Christmas Eve the sorting office was full of shrieks and singing under the paper concertina streamers. Parcels were flung about with extra exuberance, especially the ones with inexpert knots and torn paper. Some burst and I saw people put the spoils in their pockets: the odd packet of cigarettes, diary, fountain pen. It was callous thieving, because the line was drawn at anything obviously expensive, presumably

because it would be too much talked about; so the modest
gifts were the most vulnerable. Amid the snatches of Good
Christian Men Rejoice and While Shepherds Watched, little
worldly refrains occurred:

'First come, first served.'

'That's their lookout.'

'They woa miss it.'

It was plain that this theft was not common practice; it
was a custom of the season, a paradoxical free-for-all in the
heightened excitement that went with handling all these
affirmations of love and goodwill. Guilt was shrugged off.
Looted cigarettes were handed round and lit up without a
qualm.

We all fiddled our overtime, of course.

On the morning of Christmas Day the vomit of last night's
excesses was frozen on the pavements. I walked in a petrified
world. There is no time so still and so silent as first light in
an urban English street on Christmas Day, when immobility
is a religious observance. I followed my star to the sorting
office.

The boss said I wasn't to work with Mrs Gandhi; I had
to help another postwoman whose temp hadn't turned in. I
had never worked this route before. It was the other side of
the district. The woman was tall, urgent, stiff-faced. There
were three big bags of letters and parcels. I carried one on
each shoulder. The postwoman took me to a vantage point
on a corner and reeled off names of streets, flicking her hand
in their direction as if dealing cards. Then she said, 'I've
got visitors,' muttered some words that included 'brussels
sprouts', and hurried off with her one bag.

The sorting had been done by someone obviously stupe-
fied by filched drink. The letters were jumbled with no
reference to streets. After an hour I had delivered to about
six houses and had walked about three miles.

The Christmas world was coming to life. Small children hurtled in and out of doors and alleys in cowboy suits and nurses' caps. A boy was hysterical on a tricycle, and three little girls ran blind behind brilliant prams. Choirs roared carols out of wirelesses, and the incomparable Bing revolved in sizzling smells of pork sausage. I was received like everybody's lovely lad.

'Come in, cock. Your hands are blue.'

'Cock, you're a little hero.'

'Fancy, on Christmas Day.'

'You need a drop of Dad's tea, cock. In you come.'

I was dragged into a house deafening with music and cap-guns, and sat by a fire like the Royal Scot's boiler. I had tea with rum in it, a black beef sandwich like a Bible, mince pies, and egg flip in a tumbler. One bag of letters was emptied on to the table, among the greasy plates and the tea slops and the blobs of blancmange, and the family sorted them into streets for me. I had more tea with rum in it.

'Well, I think you're a hero, cock. That's what I think.'

'This'll put some blood in yer bones.'

'I 'ope they're paying yo double.'

I had more tea with rum in it.

'Our Cissy lives at number ninety-eight in Hawthorn Street. When yo get round theer, yo knock on the door and say I sent yer. Er always 'as egg flip. Yo'll need it by the time yo get round theer.'

I left one bag in their kitchen, to be collected and dealt with later, and lurched away with the other. The world brimmed with egg flip and fondness. It also reeled.

By the time I had picked up the second bag families were in their paper hats gnawing chicken legs. I felt I had known everyone around for years.

The boss of the sorting office hunted me down in a van, with an assistant. He was in a furious temper.

'Where's that bluddy woman? She's a bitch.'

I said something about visitors and brussels sprouts.

'If I'd known she was gunna swing this on yer, I wouldn't have sent yer. The bluddy bitch. I want my dinner. Do you know what time it is?'

I was totally unconcerned. The boss and his assistant took my bag and hurried through what remained of the delivery. They drove me back to the sorting office, and the boss shook his head in disbelief at the clock. He said: 'I'll wring that bitch's neck. Visitors, the bitch.'

I walked home, giggling, and arrived to a great fuss of commiseration. I ate in splendour, while the noble voice on the wireless took us 'winging, winging over the snows to Greenland'. I was a hero, like the lonely light-house men and all the other indispensable toilers who kept the world afloat while it guzzled and snored on Christmas Day.

The party was in a house in a terrace on a slope, and we occupied the front room. The front door opened straight into it. A sofa and chairs were back against the walls. There was a sideboard with bevelled corners covered in bottles of beer, glasses and sandwiches.

We piled our coats on the double bed in the room facing the top of the stairs, where it was as cold as a cellar, and crowded into the front room where the fire made our skin glow red. There were ten or twelve of us, youths and girls from fifteen up. The girls were all in new dresses, or jumpers and skirts, and all in bright colours, with necklaces and bracelets and ear-rings, and rectangular hair-dos stretching from two or three inches above their heads down to their shoulders. They filled the room with Timothy White's smells of shampoo and scent. Their lipstick was scarlet. I was the youngest but not the smallest among the lads. We wore our best suits, double-breasted, and shirts with stiff collars and

shining, wide ties. My tie had big red and white spots.
Our hair gleamed with grease. I had shaved unnecessarily.
I looked at the beer in suspicion, excited. I had never drunk
beer.

'Get some bottles open then. Come on, let's get things
going. Doa sit there like a lot of stuffed dummies.'

'Who am yo talking to? Yo doa know they all want beer.'

'Doa be mardy, our wench. We'm all drinking tonight.'

The amber bubbled and then frothed white over the rim
of the tumbler. I sank my mouth into it, and sucked bitter
foam and then cold tea without sugar, fizzing. I blew acid
splinters down my nose.

'Doa sip at it. Get it down yer.'

'Eh, he wants to tek it easy, if he ay used to it. We ay
'aving anyone sicking it up in 'ere.'

'Doa be mardy, our wench.'

I got the sequence right. Two deep gulps in succession,
breathe out hard through the mouth; be vulgar; no more
iron filings in the nostrils. I was under way.

The drink of men, the stuff of confidence and an un-
fettered tongue, the food of maturity and belonging, the
lubricant for the stiff responses, the glasses of fun.

'Yo ready for a refill? We'll be up the road for another
crate in a bit.'

'Eh, he wants to get some of them sandwiches down 'im
if yo'm gunna keep pouring that stuff down 'is gob. Yo
know he ay used to it.'

'Doa be mardy, our wench.'

The film of silk lining the head, the growth of the muscles
and the lengthening of the limbs.

'I can see yo've tekken to this stuff. We should have got a
barrel, but we day put the order in in time.'

'Eh, I don't know. Yo wait till the fresh air 'its 'im.'

'Shurrup, our wench. It's Christmas, ay it?'

The muffling of the ears, the readiness of the smile, the spontaneity of the hands around the taffeta breasts.

We had the light out and the girls sat on our knees; bracelets and ear-rings and hair glinted in the firelight. The red lips were wet, and shampoo was on my teeth. But that was all for now, although it was a lot.

The girls chattered to each other from our knees, and talked about foremen and face powder.

We all sang. I did Hoagy Carmichael — 'Are you gonna be mellow and bri-ight to night, ole butter milk sky?'

'Yo used to be a singer, day yer? I remember yo, with yer dad.'

Heavy lips, and sweet sweat in the eyes, and thighs flattened hot under a round girl.

Silent night, holy night. A gentle mist around the head, a world made of cushions and lipstick.

And abruptly it was cold, with a dusty, grey fire and busy girls doing housewifely things in the kitchen, making tea and putting biscuits on plates, while the boys peed in the garden.

We all walked home, intimate and easy in a bunch, laughing at nothing but very loudly. Where were my knees?

A kiss on the hoof and a stagger over a kerbstone, and I was taking deep breaths to scour my lungs at the back door. My head was huge and bound tight at the temples by rope. Could I get rid of this grin?

'Had a good time?'

'All right.'

'Who was there?'

'People. Goodnight.'

Bed was a wheelbarrow race.

The dance was in the Mining College hall. I went early, shoes like black glass, to show off with my new confidence in the slow foxtrot. The point about the slow foxtrot was to sustain a smooth, continuous line of movement, avoiding any jerkiness in bringing the feet together. Only good dancers could do it; I was a natural, a creature of the pop rhythms of my time.

I liked the swoop and the thigh-to-thigh partnership of the dance floor. I also liked this curious, relaxed, in-group atmosphere of the moments before the first tune, when the band practised phrases and laughed, and little groups of dancers stood round the empty floor talking about last week's fight, late on at the door, and the new pianist and today's match at the Wolves. They were moments of promise and exclusiveness.

The lights went down, the leader with the saxophone tapped his right foot on the stage, and the band was away with the introductory bars of In the Mood.

The hall filled up; the temperature and the pulses rose. The jivers claimed their rights to the four corners, with their frantic, perilous variations on the quickstep. There was brilliant invention here. A short youth with an ugly, bent triangle of a nose and straight hair flying round his ears threw his partner first under one armpit and then the other, then between his legs; he held her in hazardous, one-handed contact, their linking arms taut and their backs arched and their free hands skimming the floor; they flew together and catapulted apart, and never lost the beat. It was athletic and thrilling, always with a hint of danger. The smoochers stayed in the centre of the floor, ostentatiously aloof from the crush of bodies around them, and clasped their hands round each other's bottoms and locked themselves up in lust, for everyone to see.

I think her name was Janet. She was older than I was, but I was fairly sure she didn't know it. She hadn't been at the dance for two or three weeks, but she was there this time, tall and tight-bodied in a dress with a folded-over V-neck and her hair loosely curled without elaboration to fall on her neck. The skin was not good on the left side of her face, and the goose-pimply patch was there as usual; but it was still a special face with its oval symmetry, its soft brown eyes and a smile that asked questions. The firm body was light to hold. She was a cool, assured, troubling girl. Dancing with her made other activities in life appear coarse. I had no cleverness when I talked to her.

'You haven't been coming up.'

'No. I've been courting.' She was slightly mocking.

'You mean serious?'

'Yes.'

'I didn't know you'd got a regular boyfriend, er, fiancé.'

'He doesn't dance.'

'But you're keen on dancing. You've had a lot of lessons, haven't you?'

'I can still go dancing. He comes and meets me.'

'Are you engaged?'

'Not yet.'

'But you're going to be?'

'Yes. Are you disappointed?' She was mocking again. She *did* know how old I was.

'Well, I like dancing with you.'

'There's more in life.' She was gentle, and cool, and I was out of my depth with her. I couldn't show off with her; she knew more about everything than I did, including more about me perhaps.

I said: 'Can I have the last waltz?' I was being bold and forlorn.

She said: 'Yes, but my boyfriend will be waiting for me at the end.'

'That's all right by me,' I said. She was more concerned for my loneliness than I was.

So we parted after the slow foxtrot, which she said was lovely, and I went down to the canteen where there was coffee or orange squash. There was a big argument going on among my friends. One of them was saying angrily to another: 'Don't you ever try that on me again.'

'Try what?'

'Cutting in. In a waltz. Excusing. In a waltz.'

'What's wrong with that?'

'Not in a waltz. Never.' He was livid.

'I don't get you.'

'Cutting in. In a waltz. Some blokes would have thraped you.'

'I don't know what you're talking about.'

'No you don't, you bloody kid. You want to grow up.'

'Well, I think you're making trouble for nothing.' He was nervous, almost frightened.

'Don't you bloody start pissing me about. Cutting in in a waltz. You're bloody lucky it was me. I tell you.'

'Well, look, let's ask somebody. Ask Arthur.' He was smiling, and only half turned to me; he didn't want to admit there was a real row on his hands.

'Never mind him. It's you who needs asking. Why did you do it? In a waltz.' He was getting more belligerent. He had big fists.

'Eh, now, look, I wasn't trying . . . I mean, Christ, it doesn't *mean* anything.' He was definitely frightened.

'In a waltz? Cutting in? You're a bloody kid, the way you go on. Do that to me again, and I'll thrape you round the bloody gents.'

'Yes, well, if you feel . . . I mean, all right.'

'Yes, well piss off.'

The angry youth's name was Baden. He said to me, when the other youth had drifted away: 'What do you think about that? Cutting in in a waltz? Eh?' I said: 'You wouldn't believe it, would you?' And I made a mental note that one had to be careful what one did with Baden about.

The jiver and his dumpy, black-haired partner were doing an extraordinary tango, stretching their short legs as if straining to reach stepping stones in water. They added dramatic twists of the shoulders and stared at the distant corners of the room. It was hardly their material; they were built for the acrobatics and the frenzy. I talked to them after the tango, and they showed me snapshots of themselves in their swimwear on a motor-bike at the seaside. I had never before considered them in any other setting than this Saturday dance.

The band played String of Pearls, which I thought was the best tune ever written. The jivers were magnificent to Woodchopper's Ball. Baden was seen to be dancing earnestly, unmolested.

I found Janet for the last waltz, and she smiled her gently mocking, unspoken questions all through it. At the end she squeezed my hands, and slipped lightly through the crowd just before the band played the National Anthem.

Downstairs there was blood on the floor of the gents, and in one of the washbowls. There usually was on Saturday night.

❦ 9 ❦

Reporter

I got thirty shillings a week. My first published sentence reported that the Dr Barnardo's League of Helpers had given twenty children a tea-party at Jenkinson's café.

I fetched the editor's tobacco, two-ounce tins of Bondman, and exasperated George, the chief reporter, who was mostly patient, by failing to check the spelling of people's names and, worse still, failing to recognize the enormity of the offence. 'Curb', meaning edge of pavement, was spelt 'kerb', in this newspaper, he told me, adding that I knew what I could do with my alternatives and my dictionary; the style of the house was inviolable. I began to use a typewriter, the keys like blobs of mercury under my right forefinger.

The junior reporter who was next up the staff from me told me solemnly that 'Journalism is contacts', and with snooty cleverness that I would never make a journalist if I continued to omit the words 'during the hours of darkness' from my court reports of cyclists' being fined for riding without lights. He became a car salesman eventually. Every Thursday morning I visited the parks superintendent to collect the figures on temperatures and rainfall. I spent a lot of time leaning with one elbow on the tall shelf above the gas fire in the reporters' office longing for work.

There was little time for anyone to teach me the craft: George gave me tiny jobs concerning old people's treats, silver paper collection and fancy dress competitions at Co-op dances, and he coughed and laughed and snorted at my mistakes, and waited for me to learn and become useful. In due course I did. Inside a year I was 'Linesman' in italic capitals in the prime position on the sports page, travelling the Midlands with the town football club, and writing a thousand words a match: 'With thick fog dimming spectators' views of the farther goals, the game started at a fairly fast pace and the ball was quickly in play in both penalty areas....'

I reported council meetings, interviewed next year's mayor, refused the offer of £2 as a bribe from a defendant in a drunken driving case who wanted his name kept out of the paper, and wore a brown trilby and drank Worthington 'E' and Joules's bitter confidently....

It was the General Election. We were excited and busy towards exhaustion. Over cheese on toast, and chips, at Coggie's Palace, which was the Civic Restaurant nicknamed after the Labour councillor who made a social cause out of it, George talked with bitter detail about the poverty he had grown up with in the 'twenties and 'thirties. He had a loathing for Conservative politicians which transformed the small figure and the flushed face, with its glasses, quick smiles and nervous laughs, into a personality exuding constrained violence. It made him gasp for breath to talk about the criminality of wealth and land ownership. He knew about employers' victimization of union members, the cruel indifference of the recent past to the unemployed with families. He was outraged by the continuing fear among country villagers in the district for the wrath and whim of the rich who owned their cottages. 'They're still doffing their caps,' he said, his voice squeaking with tension. 'It's still Yessir and Nosir every other word. Christ, I've *seen* it. The other lot are going on to *win* this election. We're a daft country. We'll never learn.'

Property and Conservatism were inseparable evils. When he said 'We' he meant workers and rent-payers. It was one of the deep satisfactions of his life to report the baying domination that the local Labour councillors then held over the Tories. An employer, stripped of his membership on council committees, had recently bleated in the council chamber: 'Is there no justice?' George said to me: 'He was nearly crying, *crying*. It was *our* turn.' But he was worried about the country, and the cigarette ash showered down his tie and pullover as he shook his head in prediction. 'They'll get back, you know. We're daft, *daft*.'

George was the first person I knew with passionate responses to politics; or, at least, the first in whom I recognized them. Any discussion of politicians at home usually concentrated on who was or was not 'a gentleman'. Neville Chamberlain had failed, puzzlingly, through being 'too much of a gentleman'. My father voted Labour in the 1945 Election, my mother Conservative, without arguing. Our MP at Cannock was Jennie Lee, Aneurin Bevan's vivacious wife, and my mother said: 'I like Miss Lee, but not her supporters.' It was a censure on rough manners and impolite talk. Now here was George talking about politics the way I was accustomed to hear men talk about soccer, with snarls and implacable resentment. After telephone conversations in the line of duty with local Tories he would mouth silent curses, stretch his head back and shake both fists in the air. There would be a gulping bout of coughing, cigarette ash would cascade up out of his typewriter, he would pursue the deposits round his desk, as if playing blow-football, and then batter the offending bigwig senseless under the keys. The copy which emerged from this fury was always without hint of partiality. Facts were sacred and comment was proscribed.

We had a visit from the ultimate Conservative gentleman, Mr Anthony Eden, in whose physique, voice and style resided all the virtues of English handsomeness, as valued by the soroptimists and the townswomen's guild. The grey, striped, double-breasted suit, the grey-striped hair, the profile tilted to the applause: he was the definitive political pin-up.

He arrived at the Borough Hall in a trill of devotion which was briefly silenced, as he was halfway up the stairs, by a bellow from one of the local evening paper men, frustrated by the crush at the bottom. 'Are you going to make the same speech you made at Stone?' the reporter shouted at him, giving enormous offence. Mr Eden paused, and the profile crumpled momentarily, as if its teeth had been withdrawn by a hand up the throat, and he said: 'Er, yes.' He struck the edge of the next step as the trilling resumed.

In the back room of the Elephant and Castle, which was the meeting place of the privileged, with easy chairs, a sofa, a piano and a gramophone, a young genius from English Electric, named Brown, lectured us incontrovertibly on the country's comic inadequacies as an industrial power. We put Joe Loss on the record player, and Brown said to a barmaid, who had some vague, tragic past involving an American soldier: 'In England tennis is the prelude to sexual intercourse. In America dancing is. Shall we dance?'

Full of beer, Mike and I ordered egg and chips in the snack bar near the office. Steam covered the windows and made the walls and chairs wet to the touch; the hot smell of chip fat and stewed tea came ramming up the nostrils like a fist in a dirty dishcloth. Mike, who had replaced the reporter who was to defect to the used car trade, had the bone structure of a thin teddy bear and goggling, bottle-glass spectacles. He had an unsuitable, combative approach to life. A slumped drunk in a trench coat and farmer's boots kept muttering 'Bloody Socialists' with a lingering sibilance into his mug of Oxo. Mike, as drunk, told the girl behind the counter: 'We're going to nationalize the milk bars.' The rural drunk stood up and said: 'Them bastards are gunna ruin me. Come outshide, Four Eyes.' Mike stuck out his face on its neck of wire, and said: 'Come on, then.' The man said: 'Backbone of thish country, the farmers. You look as if a good meal ud do you good, Four Eyes.' The girl said: 'How many sugars? You can't put your own in no more.' The man sat down and drew invisible doodles above the table with his right fist. Mike sneered back on his stool against the angle of the counter and the wall, like a boxer between rounds, lucky to be still whole and not knowing it.

Aneurin Bevan came on publishing night, and the three weekly papers with similar circulation areas decided to pool resources to make sure none was left ignorant of any of the wicked magician's insults about the Tories. Bevan was the master of platform invective, the voice to breathe o'er Eden like a blow lamp. Lady Conservatives could see the horns on his head, and some of them could see his head on a plate. No-one was more quotable. We were not to miss a word. We prepared a rota system of note-taking: short bursts, the transcription to be done at the typewriter in a room at the back of the hall, messengers to rush off to the three offices with batches of copy. Within a few minutes of the end of the meeting Bevan was to be verbatim in the three editors' hands. There was a thrill and sense of importance in contemplating this rare exercise. We were charged with responsibility; in on the instant of national news.

Bevan did not help. He spoke at an unfairly rapid rate for the ones with poor shorthand and saved his leers, winks, seraphic smiles and comedian's gestures at the hecklers for those who had the best. A great fluster developed. We each had a code letter to type on our copy to keep the sequence right. The sequence went wild. There were appalling moments when the reporter's chair was unoccupied and the typewriters were over-subscribed, and there was a frantic scurry to plug the gap. The conversation made the blood run cold:

'Someone's put these carbons in the wrong way round.'

'What are these spaces in these sentences?'

'Sheets A2, A3, A6 . . . Something wrong here.'

'The ribbon's torn in that one.'

'Well, Christ, he was so bloody *fast*.'

'Don't ask me, mate. It was your take.'

Running figures sped from office to office, asking for missing sheets B8, C3, E5 . . . The editors considered some of the material to be most unlikely. Our room was cold, and we sweated. When Bevan had finished, and we were accusing and excusing with stretched mouths and bitten lips, a man from the *Daily Herald* came in, asked if he could have a look at a set of our carbon copies, extracted his three hundred words from them in about five minutes, and went back to the pub he had come from. It had a 'phone. 'Thanks a lot,' he said. 'Same old stuff, isn't it?'

Labour lost the seat to the Conservatives, along with many more. Soon after the result was declared I 'phoned a director of the football club to talk about a new player. He was a jobbing printer with his own small business, and a Labour man. He was in a spluttering bad temper, having just taken a 'phone call from a Tory who wanted some work done. The printer said: 'Do you know what he said to me? He said, "We're having a drop of champagne, if you'd care to call round." I told him. I said, "Champagne? Do you know what we're on here? Cold tea. That's what. Cold tea." The bastards. They're back. It's started again.'

George was purple at the typewriter, the ash puffing out of it as he cremated the loser.

Mike and I went to a holiday camp for a week. It was on the coast of North Wales, and there was still a strong look of

military fortification about the place, with pill boxes and
gun-emplacements streaked and rusting and split by insinua-
ting weeds. And, reinforcing this appearance, the camp had
a military life-style, with NCOs called Redcoats, in their
scarlet blazers, to marshall the queues at Reception and
Documentation. 'Hend in your reshun books . . . Keep
mewvin, puleeez.'

The campers were accommodated in long, straight lines
of chalets with double-tier bunks and wash basins and little
bedside mats sliding about on shiny floors. There were
wooden duckboards over the mud between the chalets and
the communal lavatory blocks. Loudspeakers in every
chalet, and fixed on to trees, walls and lamp-posts, sang
waking-up songs, time-to-eat songs, little-laddies'-birthday
songs and go-to-sleep songs at us in a chuckling and relentless surveillance. A Gents was a 'Lads' and a Ladies a
'Lassies'. There was not a mother in the place; only mums.
There were no children; only kiddies. We were experiencing
the frantic, dying gasps of the wartime mateyness, its in-
evitable commercialization hounding it to its end with a
clangour of tills. 'Wakey, wakey . . . Give yourself a shakey
. . . First sitting, puleeez, dohoant be latey . . . Good night,
campers, see you in the morning. . . .'

The dining room, like the rest of the buildings, was pre-
fabricated, with eight-place tables, plastic cloths, sauce
bottles, big cups and folding chairs. We sat opposite two
brothers roughly our age, named Waddington. There was no
more than a year between them, and they looked nearly like
twins, brown-eyed, well-built, with slow Northern voices.
They always called each other 'Wod', confusingly. We
settled on Wod for the older one and Woddy for the
younger. We went drinking with them on the first night,
competitively.

The camp was excellently equipped for drinking. It had

austerely functional beer-swiggers' bars uncluttered by carpets or sandwiches, a hybrid lounge with a middle-age smell of pipe tobacco and lavender water, and a fanciful Olde England cocktail bar equally suited to men in Tootal cravats and with Air Force badges on their breasts and to our lurching, open-necked selves, with our ties in our pockets. We completed the course there with lopsided eyes and wet elbows.

Wod said: 'What d'you think of these two, Wod? Right boozy pair. Bluddy reporters.'

Woddy said: 'Right boozy pair.'

Wod said: 'It can't be so 'ard, reporting, Wod. Right pair of boozers.'

Woddy said: 'Right pair. Bluddy reporters.'

Wod said: 'It can't be so 'ard. What d'you need?'

Woddy said: 'Good lina talk, Wod. Bitta push. Few jokes. Right pair of boozers.'

Mike said: 'Christ, we sound like a couple of quick-patter comedians.'

Wod said: 'Right pair of boozers.'

One of the camp photographers took our photograph as we sat round a small table whose top was covered in glasses and bottles. 'It'll be ready tomorrow lunch,' the photographer said.

Wod said: 'Dare you to send that to your boss.'

Mike said 'Won't worry me.'

'Nor me,' I said.

Mike did his deep, film cartoon voice, and said: 'We're sorry, Mr Editor.'

'Right pair,' Woddy said.

Wod said: 'We're not doing this every night. We'll be bluddy broke by Tuesday.' It was a sensible warning.

'There's a bit of talent about,' Wod said. 'Seen anything, Wod?' Woddy slitted his soft eyes and grinned, looking sensuous and oriental. 'There's a fair bit about.'

We went to the dance, grinning past the attendants at the door. It was packed, and hot, and the coloured lights, revolving in the trumpet blasts, induced in me a kind of slow-motion, dreamlike epilepsy. I reached out to grab arms and pillars, and they retreated or veered aside. I was tripped by an empty cigarette packet. The world was smiling and friendly, but impossible to pin down. Figures came and went, leaving perfume and imprecise memories of touch and movement. There was a blonde girl, certainly, and another with a doll's unreal blue eyes. Or were these two actually the same girl? There was a small, dark girl with a sharp voice, who was connected with a big, dark youth. 'I-yi-conga. I came, I saw, I congaaad.' A trapdoor opened immediately behind my heels, and I balanced on its edge to applause, hung one leg into it, climbed out again. 'And that's what I call bohowling the jack. . . .' The crystal glinting above the centre of the dance floor came loose and swung like a pendulum. If I reached up I could touch it. Who wants coffee? Never touch the stuff. The 'Lads' sign went blurred, there were hands under my shoulders, something hard struck my forehead without hurting, and my stomach emptied like a flung bucket.

The night was a cool stumble through ankle-deep sand, with a body on either side of me, and I was carrying them both. I had the top bunk, and I dived downwards into it.

'A right boozy pair, you two,' Wod said, at breakfast. We all ate the full fry-up. Our waitress was a small, dark-haired girl, with dark eyes and dancer's calves and an accent I could not place. She looked at the four of us, one by one and then looked all round again with a general appraisal, and then she looked hard at me.

'What have you got to say for yourself this morning?' she said.

I remembered dark eyes that I couldn't remember. 'Er, well, why, what?' I said.

'I'd have thought butter wouldn't melt,' she said. The accent was very troubling. 'With Nicky being a Redcoat it was all right. But, well. . . .'

'Well, it's all right then, isn't it?' I said, remembering the dark eyes and the dark youth whom I also could not remember.

'He was right blind,' Wod said.

'You all were,' she said. She was hard and pretty, about nineteen, a composed woman.

Wod said: 'What's your name?'

'Eileen.'

'Where do you come from?'

'Liverpool.'

The accent was placed, and a romantic harshness glimpsed of big ships in port, and fights with dockers' hooks.

'Have you finished?' she said to Woddy.

'Yes,' he said, looking down at a plate wiped clean with bread.

'Well, put your knife and fork together, so I'll know,' she said, and she gathered plates and cups and saucers on to a tray, and hurried away. The dancer's calves bulged just where her skirt stopped.

'That's talent,' Wod said. 'Liverpool.'

I said: 'Who's Nicky?'

Wod, who knew everything about the camp already, looked round the room, but could not find Nicky. He said: 'He's one of the Redcoats. You'll have seen him. Curly, dark-haired bloke. My build.'

'Taller,' Woddy said.

'You saw him last night, but you didn't know. He was dancing with her, and you fell into them. You wouldn't let go of her.'

Mike did his film cartoon voice: 'Sorry, Mr Redcoat.'

Wod said: 'There he is. In the shorts.'

He pointed out of the window at a tall figure in its red blazer and with brown, oval legs coming out of little white shorts. He had a gang of boys with him, organizing some ball game. He was athletic, showily life-guard looking.

'Sorry, Mr Redcoat,' said Mike.

I sniffed, and said: 'So what?'

Woddy said: 'Looks right pansy.'

'Go and tell him that, Arthur,' Mike said.

'We want some talent,' Wod said. He was looking intently round the room, nodding faintly as he ticked off faces. He said: 'The afternoon dance is the place. They'll all be there. You can get fixed up for night.'

It sounded practical. We went away to wait.

He proved right in one way, not in the other. The afternoon dances were breathless with girls; but they used the dance hall then like a club, talking in huddles, dancing with each other, practising steps. There were also family groups, parents dancing stiffly and mothers guiding frilly small daughters and blushing small boys round the edge of the floor. The curtains were drawn back. The cold daylight was inhibiting. When we danced with girls they called out over their shoulders to their friends.

Wod said we had to take a much firmer line; he thought we should stop operating in a four-man squad, and work individually. But we liked being together, particularly in the bars early in the evening. I enjoyed the ease and security of that; the pint pot was status and pleasure and accomplishment. But one night, at last, we all four left the dance with a girl each. The girls were friends. We made for the sand dunes, in a cuddle and giggle.

'How old are you?'

'Why?'

'Well.'

'How old are *you*?'

'Why?'

'Well.'

'What's it matter?'

I was following through a form of known but unaccustomed procedure, not really excited, and disappointed because of it. The girl was not the prettiest, or the liveliest. Wod, of course, had the prettiest. We kissed and breathed hard, and we heard laughing and squealing nearby in the sandy half-light. My girl was wary, inquiring. She wouldn't sit down. I held her tightly as we stood together, and ran my hands up and down her back. When I ventured them around her bottom she jerked her elbows up, and arched away. She would kiss, but nothing more. I had no skills. I was becoming bored.

There were rustlings and murmurings. Woddy appeared with his girl, arms round each other, the two dishevelled, the girl flushed and flicking her long hair. She said to my girl: 'Come on, we're going back now.'

She and Woddy walked in front, arms round their waists, faces leaning together. My girl and I did the same, and there was a feeling of relief between us. I could hear Mike's voice somewhere close. There was a fierce, shrill scream, then a padding of feet, and Wod's pretty blonde girl appeared over a hillock of sand and grass, running hard in her white dancing dress with silver on the skirt. She stopped, and waited for Wod to catch her up. He was carrying his jacket in his hand, and he put it round her shoulders with studied movements for us all to watch. They sat down together, and we walked on, back to the last half-hour of the dance, and kisses, and our neat, narrow, childish bunks.

I heard Mike come in, but let him think I was asleep. If he had a success story to tell I wasn't going to give him the chance until morning. In any case, in the self-centredness of my youth I was not much interested. I was tired, so I slept. I had taken the powdery, scented-soap smell of girl to bed with me; it was sweet, curiously like the bed of infancy, and I did not dream.

'How did you get on?' Mike said, in the morning.

'Not bad,' I said.

'What's that mean?'

'Well, you know. Not bad. Nearly. How about you?'

Mike did his cartoon voice: 'Thank you, Ma'am.'

'All right?'

'Well, not really.'

'You took long enough.'

'Well, you know. While there's hope. How about Wod?'

I shrugged.

'Woddy?'

I shrugged again.

The brothers were more oriental than ever under their beige tans, Woddy's white teeth brilliant with suggestive smiles. He searched for the girl's face away down the hall at breakfast, found it, and grinned at us in triumphant self-satisfaction. 'I'm seeing her tonight again,' he said.

Mike said: 'What was that screaming, Wod?'

'I was only trying to get her dress off,' Wod said, the voice elaborately fat and slow.

'What happened after we left you?'

'I got me hand up.'

'Dirty booger,' Woddy said. He remembered to straighten his knife and fork for Eileen.

I said: 'We sent that picture to the office.'

'Right pair of boozers, they'll think you two are,' Woddy said.

On the Friday night we spent what was left of our money, doing the full round of the bars again, and at the dance we were relaxed, exuberant, old hands among people we knew, satisfied with the fun we had had, holding no failures against anyone. Eileen was there, the first time I had seen her at the dance since that first, reeling night of danger and idiocy. I danced with her, and she was like dark, firm flowers in my hands. I was heady with drink, but my balance was sure. I had learned a little. But she did not look at me much; her eyes were sharp for the corners of the floor.

'I've got a suntan as well, you know,' I said.

'Not like Nicky's.'

'He isn't here tonight, is he?'

'How should I know?'

'I thought you were his girl.'

'Nicky's got more than one girl. Is this your last night?'

'Yes. Do you care?'

'Nicky goes his own way.'

She was hard inside, to make me feel loose and half-made. She was exciting.

She let me take her back to her chalet, which she shared with another girl. It was a room that was lived in, untidy with clothes and cosmetics: a littered intimacy, with smells of her and her friend, private and heavy and adult. It was a room outside my experience. We sat on her bed, and she was indifferent; I was hot and uncertain with urgency. Abruptly she said: 'What do you want?'

'You, I think.'

'You're not old enough.'

'Oh Christ, Eileen.'

'No, you're not. Not for me.'

I felt there was one vital move that would turn the night, put me in control. But my body would not act. She could help, but she would not. She was tougher in her little, knowing body than I was.

Desperately I tried to talk it out. I put my hands on her

round, firm-flower breasts, and said: 'These are lovely, Eileen.' I moved my hands up to frame her round, firm face lightly, and said: 'So is this.' She looked steadily back at me, hard and strong in her dark eyes, and said nothing. We sat upright, staring. I was immobile.

The door opened, and her friend and a young man walked in.

Eileen stood up, taking me with her. 'Good night, love,' she said, and her voice was harsh and careless. But then she kissed me quickly, with a gentleness that amazed, on the lips.

And with her flat hand against my chest she pushed me away, on to the duckboards and into a cool, impersonal night, where my head burned, although not for long.